AWAKENING THE DREAMER

Raechel Bratnick

*Dear Kathy,
Dream strongly,
dream wisely, dream
truly and be blessed.
Warmly,
Raechel Bratnick*

A Society of Souls Press
Oldwick, New Jersey

A SOCIETY OF SOULS PRESS
28 Meadow Lane
Lebanon, New Jersey 08833

© 2003 by Raechel Lea Bratnick

All rights reserved. No part of this book may be reproduced or transmitted in any form or by any means, electronic or mechanical, including photocopying, recording, or by an information storage and retrieval system, without written permission from the copyright owner.

First Edition

Printed in the United States of America

10 9 8 7 6 5 4 3 2 1

This book is printed on acid free paper.

Cover and Book design by Scott Wilson
Cover art © by Arlene Shulman

Library of Congress Cataloguing in Publication Data
Bratnick, Raechel Lea 1943
Awakening the Dreamer / Raechel Bratnick
Includes bibliographic references.
Library of Congress Number:2003093846
ISBN : Hardcover 1-4134-1448-6
Softcover   1-4134-1447-8

To order additional copies of this book, contact:
Xlibris Corporation
1-888-795-4274
www.Xlibris.com
Orders@Xlibris.com
19450-BRAT

A Society of Souls Press
www.kabbalah.org

Raechel Bratnick
www.awakeningthedreamer.com

FOR JUDITH SARAH SCHMIDT,
my sensitive, wise mentor who introduced me to the magnificence of dreamwork.
I am proud to be part of your lineage.

"...when you dream it's where you were born."

– Li-Young Lee

Contents

INTRODUCTION ix

PART ONE: AWAKENING

INVITATION 3
THE LEGEND OF THE SEVEN SLEEPERS 9
THE PATH OF THE CONSCIOUS DREAMER 17

PART TWO: THE DREAMER'S WORK

INTRODUCTION TO THE DREAMER'S WORK 37

1: MAKING A CONSCIOUS INTENTION 41

Living Unconscious Intentions ▪ Dreams And The Heart's Intentions ▪ The Seven Sleepers Teaching ▪ Making a Conscious Intention in Dreamwork ▪ How to Find an Intention ▪ Guided Meditation to Find Your Intention ▪ The Surprising Intention ▪ Working With Resistance ▪ How Dreams Respond to Intention ▪ A Conscious Dreamer: Julie

2: RECEIVING AND GATHERING DREAMS 61

A Right Relationship to Dreams ▪ The Seven Sleepers Teaching ▪ Finding Your Dream Rhythm ▪ Creating a Spacious Cave ▪ Intention for Gathering ▪ Keeping a Journal ▪ Initial Exploration ▪ In-Depth Exploration ▪ Resolving Roadblocks to a Fluid Dream Life ▪ A Conscious Dreamer: Alice

3: CREATING A SPIRITUAL PRACTICE 88

What is a Spiritual Dream Practice? ▪ The Dream's Transformative Power ▪ The Seven Sleepers Teaching ▪ Fundamentals of a Ritual Practice ▪ How to Create a Practice ▪ Working With Resistance ▪ A Conscious Dreamer: Liz

4: TRANSFORMING DREAMS INTO CREATIVE EXPRESSIONS 103

Speaking in Dream Language ▪ *The Seven Sleepers Teaching* ▪ *Reclaiming Your Hidden Language* ▪ *Working With Resistance* ▪ *Necessary Resistance* ▪ *Creative Choices* ▪ *Priming the Creative Pump* ▪ *Free Association* ▪ *Active Imagination* ▪ *Becoming the Symbol* ▪ *Visual Arts* ▪ *Dream Painting* ▪ *The Mandala* ▪ *Mandala Variations: The Inspiraling Mandala; The Autobiographical Mandala* ▪ *Collage: Basic Collage; Tissue Paper Collage* ▪ *Sculpture* ▪ *Mixed Media* ▪ *Creative Writing* ▪ *Free Writing* ▪ *Poetry* ▪ *Epitaphs of Dream Characters* ▪ *Meditation* ▪ *Movement* ▪ *A Conscious Dreamer: Janice*

5: INCUBATING A DREAM 154

What is Incubation? ▪ *The Seven Sleepers Teaching* ▪ *Which Dreams to Incubate* ▪ *Why Incubate a Dream?* ▪ *How to Practice Incubation* ▪ *Working With Resistance* ▪ *A Conscious Dreamer: Amanda*

6: CREATING A DREAM COLLECTION 171

A Panorama of Dreams ▪ *Finding a Thread of Connection Between Dreams* ▪ *The Seven Sleepers Teaching* ▪ *How to Create a Collection* ▪ *Transforming a Series of Dreams Into Creative Expression* ▪ *Collage* ▪ *Story* ▪ *Touch Drawing* ▪ *Learning From a Collection* ▪ *Working With Resistance* ▪ *A Conscious Dreamer: Ingrid*

7: CONNECTING WITH OTHER CONSCIOUS DREAMERS 188

The Dream Community ▪ *The Seven Sleepers Teaching* ▪ *Community Dream Models* ▪ *Working With Resistance* ▪ *Unexpected Blessings* ▪ *Creating a Dream Community* ▪ *Guidelines* ▪ *Sharing Images as a Couple* ▪ *Group Exercises* ▪ *Wheel of Association* ▪ *"If It Were My Dream . . ."* ▪ *Group Dramatization* ▪ *The Evolution of a Dream Community* ▪ *A Conscious Dreamer: John*

PART THREE: STAYING AWAKE

THE IMAGINAL JOURNEY 221
DREAMS OF AWE 234
CONTINUING THE JOURNEY 247

■ ■ ■

ACKNOWLEDGMENTS 254
FURTHER READING AND RESOURCES 256
INDEX 260

Creative Exercises ■ *Working with Dreams* ■ *Imaginal Journey and Meditations*

Introduction

Sleeping Toward Heaven

I wish that I had been one of the Seven Sleepers of Ephesus,
their cave was so quiet and their bed a dim century
forgotten till their return. Think of our time—
bells and honks, a schedule even for how to relax
for success. But when they woke up, their work had all
been finished—had transformed the whole world:

While they slept, faith flowered, an outside dream,
and surrounded them in their cave. All they had to do
was to sleep toward Heaven and open their eyes
like dolls. Up there on the ceiling was all they needed.

—William Stafford

Dreams often drop mysterious ideas into our laps without any explanation. When I decided to write about the dream process which has so profoundly fostered my growth, I asked my dreams to guide me. One night the answer came. I was to *write a dream book about the Seven Sleepers*. A mysterious fragment followed it: *the dream comes apart in seven pieces*. What were these seven pieces? How was the legend of the Seven Sleepers relevant to contemporary dreamers? Intuitively I knew this dream was important, and I must explore it with my imagination to discover what it meant. An earlier dream helped me as well. *I am leading a group, using dreams and guided journeys into the depths of the "being" into mythological places. I am using music, art, and words to lead people into the caves of their knowing. I have written all the journeys in my illuminated journal.*

My work with these dreams revealed the Seven Sleepers to be an archetypal model for the expansion of consciousness through the exploration of dreams. Just as the cave of the Seven Sleepers is a shelter for their emerging consciousness, so the cave of knowing resides within each of us. *Awakening the Dreamer* illuminates the journey to this cave of knowing. It presents the path of the conscious dreamer. Being conscious is the state of being awake and alert to all of one's self.

The conscious dreamer understands that below our surface self there is an unlimited depth. The process of accessing the deeper parts of the self is a spiraling inward through layers of emotions, sensations and levels of awareness. Many of our responses to life are reactions and defenses, which are distortions of the true self. These distortions separate us from ourselves, from one another, and ultimately, from God. The awakened dreamer seeks the true self, which is most authentic and most knowing.

INTRODUCTION

How to Use This Book

The work of awakening through dreams is supported by those who have walked this path before us. I recognize that though I have walked this path for many years and relied on others who have done so to guide me, we all have different ways of learning. For example, it has been important for me to marry mysticism to the practical. *Awakening the Dreamer* offers you a variety of ways to explore your dreams— from poetry and myth, to practical guidelines and unique ways that have inspired other dreamers.

Part One tells the story of the Seven Sleepers, first as historical myth and then as contemporary dream myth. It describes the path of the conscious dreamer through my own personal dream journey and introduces you to seven parts of the dream process.

Part Two presents the work of the conscious dreamer. Each chapter includes the flowering of the legend and describes simple, practical ways of working with dreams; thoughts on understanding and resolving resistance; and the story of a conscious dreamer.

The dreamers you will meet in this book are ordinary people who through my classes discovered previously hidden parts of themselves. They learned to honor their dreams, which they understood as a way to play and co-create with their souls. This helped them to develop their intuitive abilities. They learned that rational, linear thinking is too limited as a tool of understanding their dreams; they shifted to a more inclusive way of perceiving, one that trusts and embraces symbols, ambiguity, and paradox.

Part Three looks ahead to your life of ever-evolving

consciousness. *The Imaginal Journey* offers ways to deepen your dream experience. *Dreams of Awe* show how dreams of the Divine are helpful to daily life. *Continuing the Journey* describes the ever evolving awakening process and encourages you to commit part of your life to solitude and spaciousness in order to truly see and know your dreams for their wisdom.

I am speaking to both your head and your heart. I want to nourish your sense of the dream world. I want you to experience what dream language looks and sounds like. And I hope that you will apply the process to your own dreams and the discovery of your self. I invite you to enter the book from your strength. If that strength is your mind, work first with the practical, cognitive steps. If it is your imagination, start by reading the teaching of the Seven Sleepers in each chapter and then taking the imaginal journey of the Seven Sleepers in Part Three.

If you doubt your ability to do dreamwork, read the stories of people who have worked with me in on-going dream circles or workshops. Their styles of dreamwork are as varied as they are. Yet all have discovered their soul language and believe in the value of dreams to guide their lives.

What to Expect

My intention is to reveal the dream path to higher consciousness. Once you begin reading this book, you probably will begin to dream more frequently. Quite likely you will want to work with the exercises

INTRODUCTION

as you are reading through it. You may feel challenged as your soul urges you to engage with your dreams in a new or different way. Your dreams may seem chaotic and complex, but you will find that working with them can be very simple.

I welcome you to this deep and fascinating exploration. It has been life changing for me. It is my hope that it will be meaningful for you, as well.

PART ONE:

Awakening

Invitation

> Humankind is being led along an evolving course,
> through this migration of intelligences,
> and though we seem to be sleeping,
> there is an inner wakefulness
> that directs the dream,
> and that will eventually startle us back
> to the truth of who we are.
>
> —Rumi
> *Translated by Coleman Barks*

This book is about awakening to your inner wakefulness, the dimension of self that is always present, always aware, and always awake—the very core of your being. It is about learning to live consciously from what you come to know of that place. It asks for your full participation and trust in the direction your true self is guiding you.

Throughout this book I use certain terms—soul, true self, inner world, heart of knowing, consciousness, Godself—interchangeably. My experience of this place-of-many-names to which dreams awaken us is that it is the self linked to something greater than who we are as individuals. I understand it as connected to and part of the divine force of life. Through these pages I quote sages, poets and other dreamers for their sense of this multi-named source of great mystery. I trust that in following your dreams you will come to your own direct and unique experience of it, for one of its aspects is infinitude.

In *The Book of Runes* Ralph Blum compares the essence of the self to water. If water is cloudy, you cannot see into it. If water is clear and still, you can see into its depths. As you quiet yourself, you discover more of who you are. Without an introspective, reflective practice, you remain murky. At night in the depths of sleep, whispers of who you truly are trace their way into your dreams. The revelations that come to you in the quiet of dreams and the waking reflections that follow show the face of your deep self.

Thirty years ago I was actively camouflaging my soul with work, caffeine, alcohol, and sex, unable to hear the still quiet voice within. Yet even then my soul patiently conveyed messages I did not know how to translate. When I began to decipher my dreams, I felt such relief. Even when the messages coming through were hard to accept, I knew I was now in contact with my soul.

In the beginning I saw only a jumble of dream adventures. As I learned to understand these adventures, I uncovered an extraordinary world—one of raw beauty, wisdom, wit, horror, and triumphal vision. My inner world helped me connect the broken strands of my life and showed me the face of God. Here was the inner guide I had yearned for as long as I could remember. Here was the path of the conscious dreamer.

INVITATION

This path of the conscious dreamer unites soul and body, mind and heart. It is a path where the guru is your own soul and the teachings are your dreams. It is a path of possibility. It is a path of becoming whole.

This process of awakening is long and gradual. Like all paths of awakening it begins with your declaration of intent. You then must have the patience and willingness to enter the cave of knowing, and the commitment to gather dreams nightly and unravel their meanings. One morning you will awaken and discover that living and working with your dreams has become a way of life. You will understand that your dreams have their own expression. (The language of dreams cannot be fully interpreted through an outside source like a dream dictionary, which limits the possibilities of the dream being a vibrantly alive communication from a soul to an individual.)

We cannot talk about dreams without appreciating the soul. Dreams carry messages from the soul. Engaging with dreams is an engagement with the soul, this elusive, seemingly intangible part of being human. So what is soul? Since soul cannot be defined precisely, it helps to look at it from different perspectives.

The 13th century Persian poet Rumi gives us the simplest of definitions. He equates the soul with consciousness, "the mystery of the inner life." Contemporary poet David Whyte describes soul as "the indefinable essence of a person's spirit and being. It can never be touched and yet the merest hint of its absence causes immediate distress."

Thomas Moore, author of *The Care of the Soul* and former Catholic monk, believes it is "impossible to define precisely what the soul is [because] definition is an intellectual enterprise" and the "soul prefers to imagine," while Daniel Matt, an interpreter of Jewish mysticism, tells us that the soul emanates "from the mystery of the highest level [and] descending to this world . . . [guides] the human being through the world."

I believe that the soul desires our wholeness; it is inclusive; it accepts ambiguity and paradox. As Carl Jung wrote in *Death and Immortality*, "The soul is assuredly not small, but the radiant Godhead itself."

To become more whole we must uncover unseen and unawakened aspects of ourselves and then integrate them into our personhood. We do this through commitment and devoted work on ourselves. Every time we lie down to sleep we have the opportunity to receive the soul's wisdom. Every time we awaken, we have the opportunity to process what has been revealed.

The soul says, "Wake up. Let yourself evolve. Take the path of consciousness, rather than the path of unconsciousness. Let your dreams inform your waking life. Use your waking life to inform your dreams. No matter how turbulent your life is, your dreams come to let you know how deeply you are being cared for." In the words of Rainer Maria Rilke, "My looking ripens things and they come toward me, to meet and be met."

In addition to understanding the soul, it helps to distinguish between the soul and the ego and their different purposes in the evolution of your life. The soul is the evolving principle of each person working towards his or her highest possible development. The ego is the servant of the soul. The work of the healthy ego is to carry out the soul's guiding wisdom and to continually reveal and integrate that which lies in shadow into the whole being.

Many unnecessary difficulties in life come from the ego's reluctance to play its natural, functional part, and its unwillingness to be in the unknown and listen for the voice of the soul. The ego believes it alone must manage your life; therefore, you sometimes make decisions either based on your ego's perception of reality or on your unconscious beliefs. The unconscious stores the parts of the personality that hide in the shadows.

The soul is less visible than the ego. A felt sensibility is needed to know it. Soul is the deepest felt intimacy. As the voice of Divinity it speaks to us in a language that can only be known when we listen into the still moment. In the same way that we do not see the Divine directly, we do not see our soul face to face. But we can experience the soul's presence. For me an encounter with soul is like opening the ark, trembling with awe. It is as if I have entered the holy of holies.

When we encounter the soul, we enlarge our capacity to meet more soul. Soul is patient: It waits for us. Then, like the first flames of sunrise, it bursts into our awareness and blinds us for a moment with its beauty. But to stay open and stand in wonder before it, we must be willing and able to receive revelation and the changes that happen during the transformative process. We must learn to allow the accompanying emotions to flow without acting upon them.

The soul desires that we awaken and take our particular place in the world. Recognizing the signs along the way is part of the process of fulfilling our life purpose. Our dreams continually bring us such signs. They continually push us into the unknown.

Will you be one of those willing to venture into the unruly territory of the unconscious and the mystery of your soul? Will you let your dreams guide you? Will you let yourself be startled back to the truth of who you are?

The Legend of the Seven Sleepers

> When you wake to the dream of now
> from night and its other dream,
> you carry day out of the dark
> like a flame.
>
> —William Stafford

Background

The myth of the Seven Sleepers is one that reaches across all cultural and religious boundaries. Its central motif is that of the cave, which Carl Jung describes as "the place of rebirth, that secret cavity in which one is shut up in order to be incubated and renewed." Little known in our modern world, this legend was part of Eastern and Western religions from the third through the sixteenth centuries. It is recorded in the Koran, in the Eighteenth Sura, entitled *The Cave*. An illuminated manuscript from 1550 shows seven Sufi masters, who slept in a cave for 309 years, remaining eternally young. As the cave is the place of transformation, these sleeping masters represent the seven levels of personal development or "degrees in the transformation of consciousness." They are *asleep* until they are *awakened* or enlightened. A Christian version venerated the Seven Sleepers as saints. Roman Catholics assigned the Seven Sleepers of Ephesus their own feast day of July 27; the Byzantine Church calendar designated October 22 and August 2 as feast days. In the early thirteenth century the Anglo-Norman poet Chardri wrote a version of the tale called *La Vie des Set Dormanz*. In the 1930s a group of German archaeologists led by Franz Miltner discovered the Seven Sleepers' Church and a burial site believed to be their cave in Ephesus. In Brittany, France, an eighteenth century chapel painted with images of the seven sleepers of Ephesus is still venerated by an annual pilgrimage.

This legend was originally recorded in Syriac or Greek; it is also told in texts written in Arabic, Persian, Coptic, Armenian, Latin and the Romance languages.

One Version of the Myth

Long ago seven young men from Ephesus in western Anatolia fled to a cave to protect themselves from being martyred. As followers of Christ, they refused to make a public sacrifice to the gods. Walled into the cave, they fell deeply asleep, awakening 200 years later to discover that their country had become Christian.

There is historical basis for this legend. The Roman Emperor Decius (249-251 A.D.) killed anyone who refused to participate in the state religion of paganism. This became known as the Decian Persecution.

According to the legend, two centuries later during the reign of

Emperor Theodosius II, a shepherd awakened the young men after he removed the stone blocking the entrance to the cave. One of the men arose and went into the city to buy bread. Seeing a cross, he was astonished to learn that, while he and his friends had been sleeping, everyone had converted to Christianity. The people were equally shocked by his clothes and money. They suspected he was holding a secret treasure so they took him before a judge where he told his miraculous story. The bishop of Ephesus, the magistrates and the Emperor went with him to the cave. They were amazed to see that none of the young men had aged. They believed that God had created this miracle to prove the validity of the resurrection at a time when the validity of it was still being debated. They agreed to absolve all the bishops who had been punished for preaching the resurrection of Christ. After the young men told their story, they returned to sleep, this time to the sleep of death.

Archetypal Symbols

There is great depth in this seemingly simple myth. It embraces two archetypal symbols, the *cave* and the number *seven*. The cave symbolizes the world center, the meeting place of the Divine and the human, which is normally hidden. It is both the womb of Mother Earth and the dark place of burial. The entrance is often difficult to find or to enter. When you enter a cave, you know you are changing states of being. You have come to a place of rebirth.

In most cultures the number seven is a holy number, meaning completeness, totality, synthesis, and fullness. C.G. Jung says that because of this sacred number we know that this is a mystery legend in which the Seven Sleepers are "numinous figures" who are "transformed during sleep . . . [Their] fate grips the hearer, because the story gives expression to parallel processes in his own unconscious which are integrated with consciousness again."

The Koran describes the Seven Sleepers as staying in the middle of their cavern. In Jung's lecture on the theme of rebirth, he interprets the middle place as "the center where the jewel reposes, where the incubation or the sacrificial rite or the transformation takes place." He tells us that "anyone who gets into that cave, that is to say into the cave which everyone has in himself . . . will find himself in an—at first—unconscious process of transformation. The transformation is often interpreted as a prolongation of the natural span of life."

Thus the Seven Sleepers tale speaks of the power we have to be transformed or reborn if we listen to the wisdom of our dream. This myth can be a map of the dreaming process and the development of one's consciousness.

Looking at the Myth as a Dream

Entering dreams through the realm of the imagination is one way to learn the language of your dreams. We can look at the myth of the Seven Sleepers as a dream. This will begin to orient you to this way of being with your dreams. As you read through the chapters outlining the different parts of dreamwork, you will encounter teachings based on this myth. The following imaginal account of this myth sets the stage for each of these teachings:

Let's imagine we are dreaming about *a land ruled by an emperor long ago. There is strife and many people are afraid. The new emperor demands that his subjects worship as he does. Following his edicts means you will be safe, but false to yourself. You will have to suppress your deeply held beliefs. You resist, but are afraid of the consequences. If you don't submit, the emperor will have you imprisoned or put to death. You talk with your friends about this dilemma. Some of them share your feelings and want to act quickly. You decide to hide in a cave in the mountain, just beyond the city. Each of you will leave separately and rendezvous on the mountainside to enter the cave together. You flee in the dark of night. But the emperor's soldiers follow you; they seal the only entrance with great stones, locking you inside.*

You are trapped in the cave. Your heart races. You are close to panic. One of your friends cries. Another rages at the stone pressed against the entrance to the cave, banging his fists against it until they are bloody. Another goes mute. One screams at God. Another laughs hysterically. But among the seven of you, one is calm. He goes quietly to each of you and says, "We must come together as a group. We can pray." At first no one pays attention to this quiet brother. But he continues to speak to each of you, repeating his words over and over again. By the time he has spoken seven times, you realize he is right. There is nothing to do but pray.

So the seven of you sit in a circle. One by one, you share your fears and longings. Round and round you circle, speaking your prayers and desires into the dark cave, spiraling deeper in vision. At last one friend says, "Perhaps we have been brought together in this cave to dream our prayers."

You have come to the natural end of your prayers. You are calm. All

of you know there is nothing to do but sleep and dream your collective vision.
- May those in the world be healed by our communal dreams.
- May those we left behind be comforted.
- May those who rage and scream see beyond their fury to their buried feelings and lost words.
- May those who are mute dare to speak.
- May those who laugh and scoff learn to question.
- May those who blame God learn to take loving responsibility for themselves.
- May the world outside the cave move to a higher level of consciousness.

And so you lay your heads together in a circle and sleep. The deeper you sleep, the higher your dreams rise, until they fill the entire cave and pass beyond the great stones into the air, where they are breathed by all the people of the land, including the emperor, and the next emperor, and the next.

Two hundred years later an old shepherd finds a huge stockpile of heavy stones, the size and kind he needs to build a permanent hut on the mountainside. On his next trip to the mountains he brings his ten burly sons. They haul the stones away to build a shelter against the bitter winter winds.

When the last stone has been removed, the shepherd sees a hole in the earth. He crawls along this tunnel until he comes upon a large cavern. In its center, he sees seven people lying in a circle, their heads touching at the center. At first he thinks they are dead. But bending over one of them, he sees the chest rising and falling. All are deeply asleep. He thinks he will wake them, but he notices they are dressed oddly and worries what his sons will do when they see these strange people. He decides to leave the sleepers and return later.

After the shepherd leaves the cave, the light of the world enters. Into the still, quiet cave comes a restless breeze, calling the sleepers awake. Attuned to the subtle world after years of dreaming, they open their eyes, one by one, and reach out to touch one another. They sigh, feeling complete and content.

But there is a restless one. He leaves the cave and crosses the field towards the city. He remembers clearly the way to Ephesus, the city of magnificence. As he nears the city, he realizes he is not afraid of the king anymore. He carries a sense of expectancy in his heart, remembering his beloved city and his years of prayerful dreams in the cave. Everywhere he looks there are symbols of transformation. He is not surprised. After all, he and his friends have been co-creators of this new world.

The people in the streets are strangers. He offers them coins for food, but they do not recognize him or his strange currency. They take him to a judge, who asks the young man his story. The judge is a learned man who has read every footnote of his country's history, including the tales of the persecutions.

He calls upon the emperor and together they follow the young man to the cave, where they find the others and the old shepherd feasting on bread, wine and cheese. There is rejoicing, and adoration is heaped upon the sleepers who have dreamed the transformation of their land.

This mystery legend, once known throughout Christian and Sufi cultures, can be a guiding pattern for awakening consciousness. The Seven Sleepers become conscious partners with their dreams, remaining true to their mission to transform the world. Being locked in the cave, as difficult as it must have been, became a blessing—a place of rebirth. We, too, can meet whatever life brings us, devoted to our longing to healing our world and ourselves. We can enter into the cave of our dreams and awaken.

The Path of the Conscious Dreamer

> You can know yourself, if you bring up
> those cloudy canvases from your dreams,
> today, this day, when you walk
> awake, open-eyed.
>
> Memory is valuable for one thing,
> astonishing: it brings dreams back.
>
> —Antonio Machado
> *Translated by Robert Bly*

What is a Conscious Dreamer?

A conscious dreamer is awake and present in every moment, sensitive to the nuances of life. A conscious dreamer takes dreams seriously, loves their creativity, and continually strives to open the doors of awareness and discover the unseen self.

Conscious dreamers participate in human development. Uniting spirit and matter, heaven and earth, they manifest transformation within and without. They heal themselves and the world from the outside in and from the inside out. Conscious dreamers move more easily between modes of being; they are active or receptive, strong or soft, at the appropriate time and place.

Conscious dreamers intend to know themselves. They understand that dreams are the voice of the soul guiding humans on their paths. Conscious dreamers come to be so present in life that they are *awake* in their nightly dreams.

Conscious dreamers live on the cutting edge of becoming. They allow that edge to expand continually. Conscious dreamers trust the soul's voice and learn the language of their personal imagery. They trust the guidance and hidden transformative powers of the images that arise in their dreams and waking imaginal voyages. They search these images to understand the interior self and who they are becoming. They allow these metaphors to enlarge their view of themselves and to help them find their places in the world.

Conscious dreamers fulfill their commitments to their dream lives. They challenge their resistance to recording dreams, learn to be more consciously present in their dreams, and give life to their imagery through creative expression.

Conscious dreamers trust the ebb and flow of dreams. They allow their dreams to work on them, while they go about their daily activities. Conscious dreamers delight in being shown their dreams' hidden language. They explore this language and integrate it, developing new understanding and behaviors.

Conscious dreamers trust the deep self. They use the mind to mine the deep self's wisdom. They have faith that their own knowing will guide them to a place of more aliveness and engagement with life. They are patient with this subtle process.

Conscious dreamers remember that the demands of waking life must be balanced with their creative dream practices. As they carry out their responsibilities to their work and to others, they set aside time to reflect and create with their dream imagery.

Conscious dreamers are patient with the process. They have faith that one morning they will awaken from sleep and realize that working with their dreams has become a natural way of living.

Modeling the Path of the Conscious Dreamer

Awakening through the wisdom of dreams is an essential part of the path I follow. Growing up in Idaho in the 1950s, I had no idea that dreams were meaningful. No one around me was introspective. I believed that only the tragically romantic poets who died young had inner lives, and they lived long ago and far away. People around me believed that only crazy people went into therapy. Those in my Scandinavian-Germanic hometown valued independence, self-reliance, and determination.

I recorded my first dream in 1973 in New York City. I was 30 years old, tormented and confused. The woman who shared my office introduced me to the idea of the unconscious. (Her father was the director of a well-known psychiatric institute.) She talked seriously with me about the dream I had written down and encouraged me to begin therapy. A seed was planted: I now knew that dreams were not meaningless and that there was an inner world waiting to be understood.

This seed lay dormant until 1976, when I experienced the *est* training, one of the early programs in the human potential movement. *Est* launched me on the path of consciousness, but I needed a more delicate, noninvasive way of working to explore myself deeply. Eventually I found a mentor and therapist in Dr. Judith Schmidt, who had been a student of waking dream and imaginal work with Madame Colette Muscat of Jerusalem.

When I look back at that first dream, I am amazed to see the clarity of the imagery. I have continued to work with its core images for years. The notes I made from that dream reveal how willing I was, even then, to see my dreams as messages from my soul. Yet it has taken me all these years to know what I know.

How did my dream consciousness evolve from that first recorded dream? I began by writing down all the dreams I could remember when I woke up. In the beginning, I only shared them in private psychotherapy sessions. I also kept a journal of my feelings, session notes, and things relevant to my inner life. In the beginning I approached my dreams by trying to figure them out because my creativity was completely unavailable to me. I had been raised in an atmosphere of pragmatism, radical simplicity and fundamentalism, where all the arts except old-time church music were forbidden.

Then I attended a course on dreams taught by Dr. Schmidt and began to discover myself. Dr. Schmidt encouraged us to draw and write from our imagery. My first creative attempts were stiff and uncomfortable, but I persisted. I wrote my first story from a significant dream about a cockroach.

I recorded all of my dreams until motherhood intervened and babies took precedence over my interior life. Sleep was interrupted; remembering dreams was a spotty experience. As my children grew and my sleep was less disturbed, I returned to dreams with a new awareness, often waking in the middle of the night with a powerful dream image. Devoting time to be with my imagery, my dreams became clearer, sometimes accompanied by a clear awareness of the dream's essence.

I explored many creative media. One year a rush of poems, inspired by dark dream images, flowed out of me. I painted in pastels—images of snakes, red high-heeled shoes, penises, women coming out of the shadows, Indian guides, and shields like mandalas. I explored moving back and forth between painting and writing, using a visual medium to inspire a story and keep my creativity flowing. I learned to close my eyes while I wrote on a computer so I could reenter the dream and see what was happening.

At the same time that I was creating from my dreams, I was actively engaged in my personal psychotherapy, working hard to unravel the layers of defense that hid my childhood wounds. My dreams were relentless. They informed my therapeutic work and became part of my language of discovery. Before this, I had no language of my own to describe my experience. Other people's language didn't tell me who I was. I was skilled at being who others wanted me to be, but I didn't know who I was. Now I had my own language, and slowly I discovered my greater self.

The metaphors of my dreams describe the many dimensions of my inner life. They are unashamedly rich and incredibly direct. Some dreams are raw and ugly. They have a nightmarish quality. I value working with this disturbing imagery, because these difficult dreams reveal what I have been hiding from. These ghosts and cripples of my childhood lead to truth. Knowing that, I am willing to meet all of my dreams. I have found that shocking dreams are always balanced by healing dreams of light.

In one healing dream *I am part of a circle of committed spiritual seekers having fun*. In another, *a healer is healing himself in the center of the busy city. He is a mandala to be contemplated*. In another, *I am asked if my pure pleasure can be of service to the world*. And in another,

I dream the meaning of Noah's flood and God's covenant with me. I hear: God does not promise that floods of feeling will not come to you. They will. But he does promise that they will not overwhelm and drown you.

A few years ago, I had a series of dreams about octopuses. One led to the next until these dreams wove themselves inextricably into my waking life. My work with this powerful sequence of dreams models the path of a conscious dreamer. You will see throughout the book examples of people at other stages on the path of conscious dreaming. Here is how I work with my dreams and learn from their connections to my waking life.

One important note about this series of dreams: Not all dreams call us to the depths that this group of dreams did. At the time they appeared in my life, they became important to my process, specific to one aspect of who I am.

"The Terrible Accident"

There is a terrible accident involving two octopuses. One octopus has driven the other to the hospital because she is gray and sick. She was so badly injured in the accident that the rescue workers abandoned her and threw out her skin. A gray-haired woman had seen the accident and is holding both octopuses when I arrive at the scene. They are crawling all over her, looking for a place to crawl into.

I take the sickest octopus from her. It is icy cold. It has become both an octopus and an intestine with a head. I am desperate to make it well, yet I run into all sorts of obstacles. No one comes to help, but I keep holding it in my arms, not knowing what to do because it doesn't die. When it begins to warm up, I search for Dr. Kim. No one wants to hold my octopus intestine, but I am fond of it and know it only seeks warmth and skin. When I cannot find a doctor to heal her, I make her a set of colorful harem clothes. She loves them, even though they make her look absurd. Then my octopus and her sister go to New Mexico to live. I am happy to have found a new covering for her so she can live in the world.

This dream was so painful it shocked me out of sleep. As I recorded it, I made an association to an earlier dream image in which I was looking for a tent-mother whose skirts I could crawl into. I recognized the recurring feeling of being orphaned and looking for someone to take care of me.

To work with this dream, I sketched the octopus in her harem clothes. I realized the red and yellow harem clothes were like the false self I had once fashioned for myself, as I had surrounded myself with a harem of men. Beneath that gregarious façade I was skinless and unprotected. So in my imagination I removed the clothes and held the skinless octopus in my arms. I loved her deeply and knew she was dying. I felt helpless to save her.

I remembered how often I would find myself half-asleep in the morning, stroking my arms lightly, as if to make a skin for myself to wear when I woke up. I felt extremely vulnerable when I realized I had been yearning for a natural protection.

I visualized the wounded octopus daily. My octopus could not survive out of its natural habitat, the ocean. It needed water in order to be healed, so in my imagination I placed her in a fish tank with a wave-making machine attached to simulate the ocean. An idea came spontaneously: I should add iodine to the water. (I later connected this to my lifelong thyroid imbalance: Iodine, a component of seawater, is necessary for a healthy thyroid.) But even with the iodine and simulated waves, the octopus still felt very fragile.

One day I checked on her during my meditation. She had died. I felt completely hopeless. If I could not save this octopus, how could I save myself from my own sadness?

I carried this image to my therapist, who often appears in my dreams as the "gray-haired woman." She said, "Maybe you can revive her." This sentence changed the course of my work with this dream. My despair had blinded me. I had forgotten how to create within the imaginal world. I thought of David Whyte's poem *Faith*, in which he says, "Let this then, my small poem/ like a new moon, slender and barely open/ be the first prayer that opens me to faith." The realization that I could revive the dying octopus was like a new moon, a prayer, opening me to the faith that my deepest wound could be healed.

I vowed, "I will not let you die. I will give you life-giving waters, pools of fluids, until your skin begins to grow again." I committed to continue removing my false trappings and to live skinless, cradling this self, gently, slowly bathing her with the life-giving waters of my creative talents, until real translucent skin formed.

My commitment was soon tested. Leaving the lobby of an office building, I saw before me a white van bolting across the sidewalk, heading directly at me. Astonished, I watched it crash through two sets of sliding glass doors. I couldn't understand why the driver didn't put on the brakes. I could see his face, his eyes distant, as if he were in shock, unable to think or act. I could not believe what was happening. As it crashed through the second glass door, I turned and ran as fast as I could to get out of its path. I could not outrun it, so I leaped to the right in a sudden burst of energy. It sped across the lobby, cornering a woman talking on the public phone, coming to rest so close to her that it grazed her leg but did not significantly harm her. Afterward, the vision of the white van in the bright light and flying glass pebbles flashed repeatedly before me. I had faced the terror of death and, in that moment, chosen life.

This waking-life accident occurred when a handicapped driver in a specially equipped van attempted to pick up his crippled wife, who was standing just outside the door. He confused the gas and brake pedals. His foot heavy on the gas pedal, he froze as his van sped forward.

Two days later, having recovered from the initial shock, I painted the accident. I was surprised to see the octopus appear, standing beside my grandmother on her crutches. (From the age of two when she contracted polio, my maternal grandmother walked on crutches.) After I finished the painting, I noticed that I had also drawn my grandmother's arms to look like octopus tentacles. This presented me with a question: Was this grandmother, the most loving woman of my childhood, my connection to the healing depths of the unconscious?

Then I saw a relationship between the accident and an earlier dream that foreshadowed it. In that dream, a white car had careened down the middle of a double lane of traffic and crashed into several cars.

My childhood history includes a deeply disturbing period that is related to these dreams. Soon after my 13th birthday my already crippled grandmother had a stroke, which paralyzed one side of her body. Initially my mother quit her job at the hospital to care for her mother, but then she saw a lucrative way to save herself from the poverty she had always feared. She converted our house into a nursing home, filled with old, emotionally and physically handicapped women. My teen years and our seemingly stable family became consumed by my mother's *driving* work force. Our family life felt out of control.

A few days after the car accident, I realized that the low-level depression I had been experiencing for years had lifted. Now I was free to face what I had walled away behind this depression. New images and dreams surfaced, including an image of vomiting up a red octopus that had been entwined in my intestines.

I am in a basement corridor with rooms off to the sides. A woman is holding a huge octopus-like animal that is wet and slippery. It moves rapidly and comes apart easily. A large man with an office in the basement knows how to hold it and keep it together. I watch the two of them with the animal. Later it splits apart. Part of the octopus is at one end of the corridor, and the heart and another piece are near his office, trying to get in the door, but the man is not there. There is great concern that the octopus will die. The woman can't manage to get it back together again by herself. There are lots of other people around, but they do nothing. Seeing what is needed, I walk over to the heart and pick it up. It is large and pulsating. It's scary to hold it. Will it slip away? I realize that although its heart is very powerful, it is pulsating rapidly with fear.

Carefully and proudly, I carry it down the hallway and place it near all its many parts. Immediately they begin to adhere to one another, attaching themselves to the heart, coming back together again. There is still one small piece at the other end of the hallway. I think that there are so many pieces here, one more won't matter; then I realize it won't be whole unless I go back again and get that piece, which I do.

The man is my husband, who worked from an office in our basement at the time of the dream. For years he had held my brokenness together, but now he was preoccupied with his new business. I realize it is time for me to heal myself and not rely on him to hold me together.

This dream led to the next one. A tiny dream with octopus imagery: *the octopus is at the center of my life now, affecting everything.* My heart opened to the wounded octopus at the center of my personal mandala.

One night feeling overwhelmed by family responsibilities, I shut myself in my attic writing/art room and began a story about a little wounded octopus. I called it "Raette's Last Dance." I wrote playfully in a new journal with a purple calligraphy pen, drawing spontaneous pictures. I wrote until the flow stopped. Days later I started again. This time I wrote until I came to the dream's hopeless place. My dream solution of creating harem clothes was not the healthiest solution. I was in the middle of the journey, searching for my true healing.

I couldn't finish the story, so I began to read information about octopuses. I learned that the octopus is the most intelligent of sea dwellers, except for marine mammals. It has lost all trace of its ancestral shell. It is a curious but shy creature which hides in caves or under rocks. It can change the color and texture of its skin rapidly. It has three hearts and is very sensitive. Jungian analyst Neil Russack in *Animal Guides says,* "Considered very intelligent, the octopus is endowed with excellent sight, great flexibility of movement and an extraordinary ability to learn from its experiences." These traits helped me understand why the octopus is such a personal symbol for me. I have these same attributes, though in a less physical sense. For example, my eyesight is not physically keen, but my inner seeing is; I am deeply committed to learning from my experiences and to becoming more psychically and emotionally flexible.

To better understand this symbol I explored its meaning through many traditions and cultures. It was considered the guardian of the treasures of the depths; it represented the powers of the underworld; and it symbolized "the unfolding of creation from the mystic center" [*The Secret Language of Symbols*]. Minoan and Mycenean artists painted the octopus with arms coiled like spirals.

I consulted J. D. Cooper's *An Illustrated Encyclopaedia of Traditional Symbols* to understand the image of an octopus entwined in my intestines. There I discovered that intestines are the seat of the emotions, associated with the serpent, the labyrinth, and the mystic knot. Russack says the Greeks considered the octopus with its spiraling tentacles a symbol of the "primeval urge to creative power." Its power is for healing and transformation.

I sculpted the octopus and painted its spirals on ceramic tiles. I delighted in executing the coil of the octopus around its bulbous body much as I had felt comforted doing penmanship practice in grade school. I felt connected to ancient artists who perfected the Celtic knot, the mandala, and spiral waves.

I learned that the octopus is related to the cuttlefish. I dreamed of *a dangerous cuttlefish in a museum restaurant. From the top of the tank, it looks pink, safe and inviting, but it has a hidden rapacious mouth which devours little fish. The cuttlefish clamps onto my feet. My father pulls it off, but I still can't get away from it. Its voracious mouth and dark, depressed body terrify me. I tell the women in the restaurant that you can't escape, or be yourself, different from others, when you grow up in a homogenized town of Scandinavians and Germans.*

In an old journal I found my drawing of the cuttlefish and a dialogue in which I searched for its manifestation in my life. The symbolism was clear. *Cuttle* evokes *cuddle*, the promise of love, warmth and safety. But it hides a dangerous hunger, for the cuttlefish in the dream has a rapacious mouth. It subsists on live prey, taking them by force.

This dream revealed the damage done to my spirit, which had left me skinless and torn into pieces. It evoked my ravenous hunger and my sense of having been devoured by a deprived mother, whose childhood was so painful she refused to speak of it. Unwilling to face her own life, she expected me to live the life she wanted for herself. I was not allowed my own self-expression. Everything from the clothes I wore to the choice of my first husband came under her persuasive influence. My father did not stand up for me or for himself. He was conflicted over his own desire to be mothered, so he capitulated to her dominance. To this day, neither parent has the willingness or ability for self-reflection. Just as my dreams have revealed, I must heal myself. I desire to be whole; I am willing to wrestle with difficult places in myself.

Since dreams have multiple, simultaneous meanings, I looked at my current life to see if I was repeating this pattern. I saw that I, too, had unconsciously been living through my eldest daughter's talents. I knew this could damage her as it had me if I continued this way. So I began making a conscious effort to develop my own creative life and free both of us. I faced some very uncomfortable parts of myself as I began the work of separating the two of us.

In the past I had avoided what lay beneath the surface, believing it would devour me. I had created a powerful worldly persona and had driven myself to success. I had presented myself to the world as *sparkling*; I never let myself feel or show anxiety or fear. I had siphoned my depression into illness, entering the gray world of despair when I was forced to go to bed with bronchitis or pneumonia. For years I avoided facing this depression directly. Finally I identified it and began to search for my real needs, "my own different self." As I nourished my creative self, my eldest daughter no longer had to perform for me.

These dreams showed me the extent of my wounds and pointed the way to healing. All I needed to do was pick up the pulsating, naked heart and carry it to the scattered parts: the octopus parts would unite, healing themselves. Re-united, the octopus will spiral down into my heart, my mystic center. But I must be willing to gather every piece in order to be whole. Sometimes I am tempted to say I've gone far enough; I've repaired all I can. But my dream directs me to continue searching.

As a result of the near accident with the van, I suffered pains in my neck, back, and pelvis. I felt like a torn and fragmented octopus. I wanted to heal gently. I wanted to move easily, but I felt dried out and broken. I needed a healing environment. I found my Dr. Kim, who described my pelvis as dry, lacking fluidity.

I decided to go to Bermuda for a week to heal and become fluid alongside the turquoise sea. Before I left, I dreamed of an overweight princess. *Against the blessings of her family, she is marrying a commoner. The press is trying to learn her story, but I am the only one with access to the photos and the true hidden story. She has holes in her soul and needs time alone to heal. She wants to vomit her pain* (just as I had vomited the red octopus). *She is afraid to do it alone. I reassure her that I will not leave her. I am her confidante, writing and illustrating her story with photographs.*

In Bermuda I went to the spa, saw a sports medical doctor, and bought myself a toy baby octopus I named Raette. I walked the beach, feeling my hips as fluid. I talked to my therapist by telephone in short focused conversations that deepened my work.

I experimented with acrylics, a flowing, rapidly drying paint. I painted the pink beach with red lava-like blood sliding into the sea and the inner world of the baby octopus, Raette—swirling blacks and reds, sometimes her eye visible, sometimes hidden. I painted the accident, with three monolithic stones, blue mountains from my childhood landscape, and a naked woman kneeling over the pink octopus. I painted four women by a well, caring for the torn octopus. They had appeared in a previous dream *as members of the Well of Life, a weekly support group. They told me to drink their pure waters anytime.*

THE PATH OF THE CONSCIOUS DREAM

In Bermuda I dreamed *of a fourteen-year old girl who likes octopuses. As a little girl she thought they were moons along her street. They were her moonlights. Since then she has learned everything she can about them.* I am healing. My wounded thirteen-year-old, brought to consciousness by this car accident, had become an imaginative fourteen-year-old.

I returned home feeling quieter and calmer than ever before. Exactly where the octopus dreams will lead me I cannot say. What I do know is they are guiding me to live my life with greater lightness and fluidity. I continue to dream about my repair. *I am finding boxes with my parts in them and want to bring these lost parts together before the Divine to be healed. I hear the word "reconciliation."* Shortly afterward, I dream I am walking along a road with a group of people, speaking about the octopus. Instantly I am holding aloft a very large octopus in my right hand. It is as large as my head, a grand healthy octopus.

PART TWO:

The Dreamer's Work

Introduction to The Dreamer's Work

The dream that instructed me to write about the Seven Sleepers told me, *"The dream comes apart into seven pieces."* At first this kernel meant nothing. I had hoped my dreams would give me a brilliant map for this book. Instead I received an opaque insight which required my struggling with it in order to make it my own. That appealed to the searcher in me, so instead of throwing it away and asking for a better map, I engaged my curiosity. I trusted my soul's wisdom even when I did not understand it.

At first I explored these *pieces*. I saw them as stages of an archetypal ritual in which each station evokes the whole, such as the preparatory steps in the Eleusinian and Dionysian mysteries, or the practice of walking the Stations of the Cross. I understood that if you explore any one of the seven pieces, you come into the presence of the mystery and wonder of your particular self. Moving back and forth among these interconnected dream practices allows you to spiral deeper into self.

I was curious about why the dream specifically stated the number and not the content of the pieces. When I researched the symbolism of seven, I learned that it's a powerful mystical number representing completeness. It is understood to express the relationship between God and humanity. Seven is a combination of three, which symbolizes heaven, and four, which symbolizes earth. Our week is made up of seven days; there are seven notes in the scale, seven steps of Buddha, seven sacraments, seven deadly sins, seven branches on the Tree of Life, and seven Islamic heavens. In some numerological systems seven is the number of perfection, security, safety, rest, and reintegration. According to David Fontana's book, *The Secret Language of Dreams*, the number seven is "the number of risk and opportunity, and of the power of inner transformation."

Since seven is a number of completion, I recognized that this dream was saying, "look at the whole dream experience," just as the cycle of a week is a whole. The beginning of the Torah tells us that a different aspect of creation took place on each of six days, and that this process culminated in a receptive seventh day. Then the cycle begins anew. In a similar way, the dream experience can be separated into seven functions for the purpose of working with one's dreams, but each function contributes to the whole.

Seven aspects of dream work do not mean that each individual dream has seven parts. This clue refers to the entire transformative experience of dreaming, which begins as a solitary endeavor, is enhanced by a dream teacher or partner, and ultimately expands into a communal experience.

The conscious dreamer trusts the process of awakening consciousness and engages in the work of dreams:

INTRODUCTION TO THE DREAMER'S WORK

1. Making a Conscious Intention
The work of a conscious dreamer begins with intention. This is the point of focus that directs you to your heart's goal. It is your spiritual commitment to yourself.

2. Receiving and Gathering Dreams
The conscious dreamer creates a receptive atmosphere, and upon awakening records what has been received. Without a recorded dream, either in writing or on tape, the dreamer has nothing concrete or the dream rapidly fades away. The dreamer then reviews his life to find what the dream is addressing.

3. Creating a Spiritual Practice
The conscious dreamer listens to the dream to uncover a simple practice or ritual to further his dreamwork. This practice deepens the dreamer's connection to the soul. It continues the dream and helps reveal its hidden meanings.

4. Transforming the Dream through Creative Expression
The conscious dreamer deepens her relationship to the dream through a creative expression. The dreamer may dialogue with dream characters, draw and paint symbols, or make a mandala, collage, or sculpture. The dreamer may write a poem or a song, a story or a play—or dance the dream. The dream and the creative expression form a complete cycle, the pulsation of spirit and earth, earth and spirit. Dream is a gift from spirit and creative expression is an earthly gift.

5. Incubating a Dream

A time of incubation allows dream knowledge to naturally come to fruition. All seeds must lie undisturbed in the earth before they sprout. Letting go of one's dreamwork, the conscious dreamer trusts when to renew active engagement with the dream.

6. Creating a Dream Collection

The conscious dreamer begins to recognize the dreams that share a theme or resonance. Collecting dreams that carry the same thread helps clarify what the soul is saying. The dreamer explores this series of dreams mentally, intuitively, and creatively.

7. Connecting with other Conscious Dreamers

The conscious dreamer, personally enriched by dreams, joins with other conscious dreamers. This takes different forms, from meeting with an organized dream group to sharing dreams, spontaneously, with family and friends. The dreamer trusts in collective soul work and the sharing of a vision larger than the individual's.

1

Making A Conscious Intention

At Lascaux

It came into my mind that no one had painted
there deep in the ground: if I made a beast,
an arrow into the heart, then aboveground
it would come into my mind again, and
what I hunted, wherever it was, would fall.

Now where I go, daylight or dark,
I hold something still. Before I shoot,
whatever the bow does, and the arrow, and I and
the animal, all come true down deep in the earth:
all that I am comes into mind.

—William Stafford

Understanding intention is a challenge for most people because they mistake it for or simplify it as will. Actually intention arises from one's mystical roots. There is a deeper mind than the one that lives in the brain. This is the heart of knowing. It resides in the ground of Being that we are. It speaks the voice of the Divine. Intention arises from this heart in a quiet inner voice that expresses our deep desire and purpose. It exists to help us fulfill our lives. To enter this process we must listen for it.

Intention is related to the Hebrew concept of kavannah. Martin

Buber, a renowned Jewish thinker, said kavannah "is the mystery of a soul directed to a goal." Intention comes from the soul's yearning for wholeness. It desires that we become our own distinct and complete whole self.

Intention is from Source, not will. It is also focus and aim, the heart's design and volition. William Stafford understood the purpose and impact of the heart's intention so clearly in the poem *At Lascaux*. "Now where I go, daylight or dark, I hold something still. Before I shoot [the bow, the arrow, the animal and the poet], all come true down deep in the earth: all that I am comes into mind."

The process of aligning with your soul's intention or kavannah is an interactive one. Kavannah, the desire and movement toward unity and wholeness, is ongoing, even when we are not conscious of it and seem to be moving in the opposite direction. Our part is to seek to understand the nature of creation and to participate in it as consciously as possible. We choose to use our divinely given free will to align with our soul's divine will. This is the first and continuing work of the conscious dreamer. This interactive process is the thread that runs throughout the dreaming process.

This chapter is about the connection between the soul and dreaming: how dreams carry intention and how we can make conscious intentions in our dream and waking lives. There are steps you can follow to help you make an intention from the ground of your being and then manifest it in your outer ego life.

It is the nature of intention to be made manifest. While intention is not synonymous with will, will is vital for carrying out intention. There is right use of will and wrong use of will.

1. MAKING A CONSCIOUS INTENTION

Often the will is misplaced and becomes a forcing current. An intention cannot be forced, but it can be made. It seems paradoxical to make an intention, especially since it arises rather than being willed to appear. But the making is done with desire and the act of listening, then speaking what has arisen from the birthplace of knowing.

Living Unconscious Intentions

When we do not listen to our heart consciousness, we live out the limited intention of the ego and the hidden intention of the unconscious. We often want the opposite of what we have; yet we are helpless to make this happen. The ego and the unconscious are at odds with our deepest hopes and desires. And yet their unspoken words create our reality. An important part of working with intention is to reveal and give voice to these unconscious expressions.

Before I understood how afraid I was of seeing the truth of my childhood, I lived out my ego's intention to stay safe at all costs. I was driven by my unconscious will. I could not say no; I never stopped working; I treated everything as top priority. Like many people, I valued myself by my accomplishments. But I was starved. The rational mind does not feed the spirit. Writer Anne Lamott in *Bird by Bird* tells us, "You get your intuition back when you make space for it, when you stop the chattering of the rational mind. The rational mind doesn't nourish you. You assume that it gives you the truth, because the rational mind is the golden calf that the culture worships, but this is not true."

When I began to listen to my heart's intention, I discovered my vulnerability. I found artistic play and my intuition. I learned how to prioritize from the heart's voice rather than the dictate of the will. That meant honoring the non-pragmatic, as well as the pragmatic. Among the changes I made was to build a studio away from the house, where I could create for the sake of creating as well as give support to others on their personal journeys.

All of this can be disorienting, but as Nietzsche said, "One must have Chaos in one's heart in order to give birth to a Dancing Star." It is from this formless chaos that intention appears.

Dreams And The Heart's Intentions

Our heart's intentions come to us in the stillness of the night and in meditation or quiet time. Dreams are one of the clearest ways to hear the heart's intentions. They bring us possibilities and potentialities for becoming who we truly are. *Possibility* is another word for the limitlessness of intention.

It is not always easy to hear intention in a dream. Often we need multiple dreams to reveal the full kavannah. The heart is very patient. It keeps bringing us dreams until we make the connection.

Recently I had numerous dreams about my resistance to being embodied. They showed me that when I suffer betrayal, I can choose to close my heart to my suffering, or open it by allowing myself to feel my brokenness and to weep. The mind does not weep. Only by descending into the body and entering the heart can we experience

1. MAKING A CONSCIOUS INTENTION

our humanity. This level of the kavannah of being human is not easy to hear in day-to-day life, so my dreams carry forth this deeper intention.

As I was working on this chapter, I came across a dream I had 15 years ago. In this dream, *I was told that nihilism* (belief that life is meaningless) *grows when a child's desires remain unsupported.* The dream went on to describe that *in the face of evil's strong power to destroy everything in its path, you must align with God/goodness and be bathed in God.* This will bring about an immediate change and help you to escape the power of evil. Certainly this is a strong dream, confronting the reality of the world. Its intention is clear: Go the way of goodness even in the face of evil. Dreams push us towards greater consciousness.

Dreams also require our trust and courageous willingness to follow them. What helps in that process is to know their source. Coleman Barks has been translating the Sufi poet Rumi since 1976. In *The Soul of Rumi*, Barks tells us, "Rumi says wherever the soul goes at night, that is our true home!" Rumi says to the Divine, "You don't sleep, but you're the source of dream vision, a ship gliding over nothing, deep silence . . ." This greater Beingness sources nightly dreams.

Knowing intention, making intention, and listening for intention are related. In fact, to want to know intention is itself an act of intention: To listen for intention is an intention. Attuning to "the intelligence of the heart" is an act of intention.

The heart's intention changes as we change, but it is always moving us toward a more whole, a more real and honest life. It is ongoing. We can choose to listen or to miss it. Listening for it and then following it is the conscious way. It is the way of knowing.

The Seven Sleepers Teaching

The legend of the Seven Sleepers begins with their declaration of intent. In the Western version, the young men refuse to worship pagan gods. They declare their commitment to one God. They refuse to adopt the language and symbols of the Emperor's religion. In the Eastern version the Sufi masters set their intentions to the task of dreaming the same dream, declaring their desire to live in Oneness on a higher plane.

As we reenter the myth through our imaginations, we listen with an inner focus for the quiet voice that distinguishes itself from our ordinary consciousness. We hear our desire to be true to ourselves. We search for the clearest way to express that desire. When we recognize the words of our deepest knowing, we set our intent. We have heard what our soul work is. We then open to receive spiritual help to carry forth this intent.

The cave of the Sleepers appeared thousands of years after the first cave art, yet it is reminiscent of those ancient caves. Paleolithic cave art reveals that the practice of intention was not separate from being. These people lived a dreamlike consciousness.

Archeologists have discovered many caves with art in southern France and northern Spain like the one at Lascaux which William Stafford wrote about. According to Van James in *Spirit and Art*, these paintings were part of shamanic practices and initiation rites. Here spirit visions of "divine-earthly creatures" revealed their secrets, their "great sacrifice . . . in order that humanity might be free to evolve to its highest potential."

These places of shamanic ritual were often far away from tribal villages. The village sage, other leaders and initiates made long journeys to these pitch-black caves; once there they often had to crawl through low tunnels to reach a larger cavern at the back of the cave. They carried paints and torches and would lie on their backs to draw.

These rituals also may have been intended to bless the group's hunters in the caretaking of their people. Some cave paintings show spear marks, suggesting the hunter's intention for a successful hunt. However, they were probably not intended for a specific kill, since the journey into the cave required a lot of planning and time.

When we consciously set aim like the Paleolithic shaman and the Seven Sleepers, we guide our journey and carry that desire into our lives. When we don't declare our intention, the unconscious will step into the gap. We are left to live out the voice of the unconscious opposition.

Making a Conscious Intention in Dreamwork

Making a conscious intention is the first step in dreamwork, but it is also appropriate to do at any time during the process. Like a marriage vow, it can be renewed often. It begins at the edge of dreamwork, when you commit to remember and record your dreams. It becomes even more active when you sit down with the dream(s) you have received. There, listening to your heart's desire, you can quietly state what you want to know about this dream. It may be as simple as the desire to know what the dream asks of you.

How to Find an Intention

Making an intention is an organic, interactive process. These steps will guide you in making an intention from the heart of knowing and will help you carry this intention into your life. They are applicable to asking for a specific dream to help you, as well as helping you understand the intention your soul has for your life.

1. Ask your wisest self for its intention. In this moment what is my clearest desire? What do I need to know about this dream? Or, what do I need a dream for?
2. Wait. Listen. Receive your heart's intention. Listen with an open mind.
3. Do not judge or reject what arises. It may not be what you had in mind.
4. Consider your intention. Will it harm me? Will it help me grow, even if it requires a risk? Is it for my highest good? If it feels negative, release it, take several breaths and wait to hear your wisest self speak again.
5. Accept the intention that comes to you.
6. Put this intention into words. Write it.
7. Allow it to reverberate throughout your being.
8. Speak it aloud.
9. Allow this intention, and the possibility of grace, to guide you.

10. Manifest this intention in the world through a creative expression or action.

Guided Meditation to Find Your Intention

You may wish to use this guided meditation to begin the process of asking for an intention. If you record this guided meditation, you will be able to follow it more easily.

"Close your eyes. Come to your breath. Let your breath breathe you. Be with this natural flow of breath. As you breathe, notice if you are feeling any tension. Breathe into that place. Slowly allow your breath to take you deeper, to a calmer place, to a place in the very center of your being. Come to the center of your being, to your source, to the place where your soul resides. Trust that your breathing takes you there. Let go of figuring things out. When you come to this quiet place, ask yourself, 'What is my focus for my dreamwork today? What direction do I need now?'

"Wait until the answer arises. Let it come spontaneously. Don't try to find it. Wait gently. You may see an image. If so, let the words of your intention form from the image. Take as much time as you need to form your intention. When you know it, speak it clearly to yourself. Give thanks for this connection with your deepest being. Then slowly open your eyes. Record your intention on paper. Speak it aloud three times. Let its wonder fill your heart. Know how this intention will carry you towards your heart's desire."

The Surprising Intention

Intentions that arise from the soul are often surprising. This meditation may totally change your expectations. When you have quieted your active mind and are listening with an open mind, you may wonder at the words of desire that come spontaneously into your awareness. What you hear may be the last thing your mind would have chosen. But this is the desire of your heart, and it deserves to speak and be listened to. There is a great awareness coming from this quiet, deep voice. It speaks what you really need, not what you think you need.

This is the experience that those of us who have journeyed into caves displaying Paleolithic art have had. After walking deep into the earth through an inky black darkness, we stand quietly in a cavern and suddenly, as a lantern is flashed upon the wall, we gaze upon primeval images which Van James says "bypass our normal, everyday consciousness." So it is to enter the silence and await the essence of your Being to shine its wisdom upon your consciousness.

Working With Resistance

Resistance to Dreamwork

When we begin to work with our dreams and inner imagery, we encounter barriers to facing ourselves. When we are blocked and cannot hear, we first need to clear away our psychological debris and sit to listen again.

We each have our own style of resistance and at the same time we share in society's distrust of the intangible. We have grown up

1. MAKING A CONSCIOUS INTENTION

focused on the "how" and "why" of life. How do you make this? Why does this work that way? What is the cause-and-effect relationship? Our education is founded on investigation and analysis. Rarely is the unexpected honored; even the arts are usually taught in a linear, step-by-step manner. The extraordinary Einstein valued imagination over the ability to accumulate knowledge, but most scientists and educators emphasize knowledge over imagination, so our thinking has been molded in this way from kindergarten through adulthood.

Most of us unthinkingly rely on facts. If an idea can't be supported by facts, we deny its validity. We rush to doctors, take medicine, read studies, put our trust in machines and industrial products. When they fail, we become angry and want to file a lawsuit. We turn automatically to sources outside ourselves to solve our problems. We doubt the transforming power of imagination and dreams.

Learning to think and discern is very valuable: It contributes to our advanced technology. But we rely on thought so much that we are unbalanced and distrust the still small voice inside. We may sense that something is missing, but we rationalize this vague feeling: "I'm not artistic;" "I have to make money;" "That's a waste of time."

When we approach dreamwork, we may discover an initial distrust for its special kind of knowing. Dreamwork loses its vitality and power of transformation when we limit ourselves to analysis. Approaching dreamwork in the same way that we approach the rest of our investigations will deprive us of the riches of exploration.

Imagery comes from our silent depths like plants that grow unseen. When we plant a garden, we hold the seeds in our hands. We can see the rain and sunshine necessary for their growth, but while the seeds are sprouting, what goes on in the earth is hidden. Still, we know the seeds rest in the earth, germinating.

We must develop this kind of trust in dreamwork. Our imagery is powerful: It can transform and heal us. But we must make this process conscious. We must plant the seeds, water and weed them, and give them time to come to fruition. We do this when we respect our imagery and quiet our doubtful minds.

When we feel resistant, we may want to acknowledge this sensitive place and proceed gently. At other times, we may want to have a dialogue with our resistance.

Here are some helpful questions to ask of your resistance:

What are you feeling?

What is your name?

What are you protecting?

When you can respond with caring to your resistance, you will understand it as just one voice inside you, not all of you.

You know you are near the treasure within when the guard of resistance is growling. Let's say you've just read these questions and are saying to yourself something like, "I'll think about dialoguing with my resistance later. It's a good idea, but . . ." and the rest of the conversation slides away into oblivion. Often the guard against awareness and change is background thought, or sensations like sudden sleepiness or hunger. As it becomes foreground, watch it take the form of a seemingly legitimate task like the need to make a list of all the things you have to do.

1. MAKING A CONSCIOUS INTENTION

Resistance to Working with Intention
The rational mind does not understand the heart mind. The rational mind thinks of safety in terms of protection. The heart's desires may threaten the rational mind. Sometimes we try to complicate what we are hearing from our hearts in order to satisfy the rational mind, even if what we are hearing is a simple statement. When you find yourself with a lengthy statement, try rephrasing it more simply. Try using a verb phrase. The verb is the active component of our language. It will help you move your intention into your life.

My intent is . . .

to know the little girl/boy in me.

to hear the whispers of my deep knowing.

to listen to the voice of my sadness.

to open to my creativity.

Resistance often disguises itself as an intention that sounds good, but may not be best for you at this time. There is always a part of us, sometimes called the lower self, which intends not to hear the truth. When we ignore the truth or want our own way, we act out this lower self, rather than acting on our soul's will and the Divine will.

If you are having doubts, check how you feel when your intention arises.

Does your breath stop?
Are you surprised by what you hear?
Does it represent a cutting edge for you?
Is it connected to what you are exploring in your life?
Does it continue your personal work?

Do you feel attuned to this intention, although it may require a risk to manifest it?

How Dreams Respond to Intention

Dreams responded to my intention to write this book: I asked for a dream to reveal its nature. I did not have the dream of the Seven Sleepers the first or second night I asked. I don't recall how many nights I waited, but every night I restated my intention, requesting a dream to guide me. Then the dream came, waking me in the middle of the night with its mysterious answer.

At the beginning, before intention becomes an integral part of your life, you have to remember to practice it. Eventually you will be able to practice intention even in your dreams. At the same time, the act of intention brings you into the present and must always be made conscious.

One of my intentions toward my dream life is that I will take my dreams seriously. Recently I awoke in the middle of the night with a short dream: *I am looking at the cover of a book titled Without Story. I wonder who I am without story.* The act of dragging myself from sleep and writing down this dream was intentional. As I returned to sleep, I wondered about this question—who am I without story? An hour later, I awoke with the dream answer: *Christ, journey, love.* As a storyteller, I can be distracted from being present in the moment without a story. This dream addressed this unconscious habit. If I did not intend to listen to my dreams, I would have discarded this dream as inconsequential. Instead, I felt inspired to reset my intention to live this

1. MAKING A CONSCIOUS INTENTION

message of being who I am, one on a journey of Christ consciousness, the consciousness of love.

A Conscious Dreamer: Julie

Julie is a healer whose intention has been to receive the messages in her dreams. Before she decided to record them, she only remembered "the big ones." Now she hears a voice during the night that tells her to get up and write them down. "I keep a tape recorder by my bed, and a journal and pen with a light. It has to be easy for me.

"When I began to record my dreams, the veil between this life and my dream life became thinner. As I work with them consciously, the veil becomes even thinner. I chant and meditate every morning, and pieces of a dream will often come back to me. Sometimes I write after I meditate. I now live my life knowing there is more going on here on earth than it seems. Working with my dreams has made me realize everything is not as flat as it used to be. I feel more connected to living. I feel richer. I lived a lot of my life in pain, so it was very hard to be conscious. I'm more awake now."

Julie came to me for a four-day, personal intensive. She brought her intention to work with her dreams and her unconscious. She wanted to have a better understanding of her fear of her dark shadow side. She believed her hate feelings could kill. "I have a wellspring of strength in my belly, but I'm not releasing it. I am so fearful that I'm living at thirty percent of my potential. I want to go through the portal of fear into this wellspring of strength." This last statement, which came from her heart and soul, became her intention for the intensive.

Together, Julie and I decided that the theme for her intensive would be the descent to the underworld to meet the goddess within. We chose the ancient myth of Inanna, the Sumerian Queen of Heaven, to embody this theme. In the myth Inanna descends to the underworld to meet Ereshkigal, her dark sister. When Julie was only a few weeks old, her mother was hospitalized; this experience, and other traumas during Julie's upbringing, left her afraid of the dark aspects of humanity.

Julie's intensive began with her preparation for the descent. The night before we met, Julie had dreamed she was a pregnant woman, lying on a rock in the middle of open space, with earth all around her. In the first session Julie birthed herself. Going through the darkness of the pain, she became a resting flower, connected to its deep roots. After the session she rested in a garden, where she painted a collage with mud and leaves and flowers.

Throughout the intensive, Julie's dreams and her paintings informed the work, leading her like Inanna to face her dark twin sister Ereshkigal. One night she dreamed of a dark, ugly room where a monster man, sitting on a bloodlike reddish-brown sofa, wanted to grab her breasts, and the sofa threatened to engulf her. In her work with this dream Julie first imagined herself as the monster man; then she threw back her head, her hair flying, and roared with the voice of the violated woman. Before the intensive she had expressed her desire to be able to roar like Ayla, the main character in Jean M. Auel's *Clan of the Cave Bear*. Because Julie had stated her intention, this dream brought her the opportunity to roar with rage in the face of fear. When she stepped into the dream, she could feel the anguish of Ayla and countless other abused women through time, including Ereshkigal.

Each day's work clearly showed her deepening consciousness.

On the second day, the theme was "Embodying the Beast Within." On the third day, it was "Facing the Destroyer and the Descent." That day, Julie brought the paintings she made after her experience of roaring as Ereshkigal, one made of bark and leaves, the other an abstract mandala. I took her on a guided imaginal journey of the Inanna myth. After the session, I sent her to a local nature preserve named The Great Swamp, where she painted and wrote a poem to herself.

On the last day, the theme emerged as "Appreciating the Fullness of Life." The night before she had dreamed of seven naked men painting watercolors on a porch. She told them that she had never seen anything more beautiful than the sight of them. One mocked her in an easy way, and she laughed with him. The dream switched, and in the new scene she was sitting on a green horsehair sofa, which was stiff, but supportive and very comfortable. This dream revealed the transformation Julie was undergoing. Where once a monster had wanted to grab her, there were now seven beautiful naked men painting watercolors, just as she had painted in the gardens. The sofa, which had wanted to engulf her, was now supportive.

Julie, like Inanna, had made the descent and returned. We explored how to take this new energy into the world in a practical way. At the end of the intensive, she spent two hours at a nearby arboretum, rejoicing and feeling her oneness with the earth. "My intensive was like a dream. Everything was connected—the gardens I visited, the dreams, even the shit that I found on the toilet in my hotel room the night I arrived."

Julie had also transformed her fear of the earth and of the bugs crawling in the dirt. Before the intensive she was much more comfortable in a city environment; during the intensive, she became fascinated with the tiny life crawling beneath her feet.

After the intensive Julie had several dreams of snakes; in the dreams her husband liked the snakes. The snakes were, in turn, fascinated with her husband, but Julie wanted to get away from them. She said, "I didn't fully understand these dreams until I reread the myth of Inanna for my thesis. Sylvia Brinton Perera, in *Descent to the Goddess*, describes the various endings to the myth. One ending is that Inanna's betrothed, Dumuzi, asks a god named Utu to save him by turning him into a snake. Utu does this and Dumuzi gains the serpent wisdom 'that nothing in the Great Round dies.' I'm still working on these dreams, but what is interesting to me is my association with the snake as Shakti, the coiled snake that is Kundalini energy. In my dreams I want to hide from this energy.

"In a way, I am levitating above the snake. About six or seven years ago I dreamed of my spiritual teacher, Gurumayi, dressed in Tibetan clothing and looking very old. She gave me three tests. The first was snakes. I passed this by levitating above the snakes. The second test began with a curtain going up, and behind it two men, one old and one young, are running towards each other out of a dungeon. They are a father and son with great love for one another. They are about to embrace when the floor goes out, and they fall into another dungeon. In the dream I told Gurumayi I can't do this. The third test was about Satan. Gurumayi said, 'Satan is going to come out of this door in front of you, and you should move to the left.' I'm acting unafraid, though I really am frightened. Gurumayi says, 'Do you know what Satan is?' I say, 'I don't want to talk about it'. She asks again. As she begins to tell me, I wake up."

When Julie shared her dreams of snakes after the intensive, she told me this dream of the three tests. She was certain she had passed the snake test by levitating. Remembering what we had been working on, I asked her, "Are you sure you passed the test? What about becoming the snake?"

Recently Julie told me, "When you asked me that question, it startled me. I realized I am still scared. It reminds me of an earlier dream in which my mother and I were walking on top of a church dome because the city below is on fire. When we descend into the chaos, people want to kill me. I have been living either on the dome or down in the chaos. This dream feels as though it described what I am here to work on in this lifetime."

Julie's style of working with her dreams is to set her intention and then wait patiently for the revelations. She may have to wait a long time, but eventually the dream unfolds its meaning. "When I don't know what the dream means, I know the answer will eventually manifest in my life. A realization will come to me while I am meditating or walking, even months later in another dream, or when someone says something to me that I recognize as the key to the dream.

"It helps me to paint, dialogue or write poetry with my dreams. Doing this brings the dream and me into the present. Otherwise the dream is an ethereal thing. I've come to see that my whole life is full of metaphor. As Gurumayi said, 'This life is a dream. When you die, you will wake up.'"

2

Receiving and Gathering Dreams

> As long as you need a dream, it waits in dream space.
> It is up to you to retrieve it.
> When you are tired and restless and wait too long,
> the dream retreats, but it never vanishes.
> It retreats to the womb of dreams, waiting.
>
> —Dreamed by Raechel Bratnick

A Right Relationship to Dreams

Dreams are elusive. They seem to emerge out of nowhere and disappear as quickly as they come. They are not tied to earth, as we are. They have no boundaries and no ordinary time frame. There are no natural transitions between events. Two people may merge into one person, or exchange identities. In dreams we can do the impossible. We can be free of physical handicaps. We can fly. The absurd is the norm, yet dreams often feel more real than our waking lives. Some spiritual teachers have suggested that the dream world is reality and our waking world is the dream.

Dreams have an otherworldly feel to them, which is why many ancient cultures believed that dreams came from outside the person—from demons or the gods. Few of us accept that belief anymore. While the exact source of dreams remains a mystery, we can definitely say that when we dream, we are in relationship with an unknown part of ourselves that is deeper, wiser and more imaginative than our ego selves are. This deep place is not visible or tangible or known to us, but we can feel it and sense its presence.

Dreams call us to reflection. They seldom give us a lucid message, although conscious work can produce clearer dreams. Even when our dreams seem obvious, they carry messages on several levels. It takes attention to discover each of these levels and practice to appreciate several meanings in the same dream.

In some cultures dreams were once considered vital for the health of the entire community. In the Greek and Egyptian worlds curiosity about dreams led to dream interpreters, dream dictionaries, and shrines for incubating dreams and divination. These shrines had specific protocols for purification rituals. The prophet Muhammad had a high respect for dreams; he created the Islamic religion from a prophetic dream he received and made sharing dreams with his disciples a part of the daily ritual. From one of his disciples' dreams, he established adhan, the daily call to prayers.

Today in most parts of the world, the communal aspect of dreams has disappeared. Those who do explore their dreams understand them as private poems filled with personal symbolism. Although the communal aspect is not of primary importance in the Western world, the act of dreaming is considered vital to the individual's personal health. Scientists have documented that without dreams, one's mental health is in jeopardy. So dreams are valued as part of psychological health, but are not valued by the general public as a means of receiving personal and collective guidance. This means that as an

2. RECEIVING AND GATHERING DREAMS

individual searching to work with your dreams you are unusual in our society.

We begin the process of gathering our dreams by learning how to receive them. We must come into a right relationship with them. We must learn to give them honor and respect.

Dreams have the qualities we assign to the right brain and its activities—music, art, dance, and poetry. Since dreams are otherworldly, mysterious, sensory, multi-dimensional, symbolic, elusive, and not bound to earthly time and space, what is a right relationship to them? Imagine a person you love with these qualities. If you demand that this loved one be logical, orderly and linear, would you be creating a harmonious working relationship? I suspect not.

If I imagined my mate with these qualities, I would want to approach him kindly without judging or trying to change him. I would create a place where we could meet quietly. I would promise to reflect on his words and listen for their deeper meaning. I would deal with my resistance. If he disappeared, instead of yelling at him I would tell him I long for him to return. I would wait patiently for his return and focus on righting my own intentions toward our relationship. I would play with him when he returned.

When I was having difficulty remembering my dreams, I dreamed of a woman dressed in white fleeing through a doorway with my dreams in her arms. I was desperately reaching out to stop her, but she was beyond my grasp. As I worked with this dream, I realized I could not force myself to remember my dreams. So I relaxed and accepted the current state of affairs although I felt sad to wake up each day without the gift of a dream. When I began to recall my dreams again, I was more aware of the conditions I needed to remember them easily.

People who cannot retain their dreams make a typical mistake: They ignore their sensations and feelings upon waking and the snippets of imagery that do filter through. The snippet is the doorway into the dream. It is the place to start. Entering it with imagination, the dreamer will find wide vistas beyond.

The Seven Sleepers Teaching

What can we imagine about the Seven Sleepers and how they related to their dreams? The cave became a container for their dreams. They chose to sleep, not to plot or dig their way out of the cave. They lay down together and opened themselves to a higher level of creation. They entered the source of imagination, which is the heart of creativity. They surrendered their egos, and they dreamed; sometimes it was only a shadow of a dream. But they wove these pieces together until their dreams filled the cave, a quilt of devotion, overflowing into the sleeping world beyond the cave. Still they dreamed on, until the dreams of every sleeper in the land were so full of possibility that their dreams spilled into waking life. Slowly the visions of the Seven Sleepers transformed the world.

Finding Your Dream Rhythm

Our ancestors slept according to the rhythm of the sun. They rested or slept from sundown to sun-up. In northern latitudes when winter nights were long, they might do this for fourteen hours or longer. During the short summer nights, they slept far less. With the advent of electricity artificially illuminated environments were created. Working and playing in these, regardless of the rhythms of day and night, we change and control our natural sleeping rhythms. As a result, most Europeans and Americans are continually sleep deprived.

Thomas Wehr, chief of the Clinical Psychobiology Branch of the National Institutes of Mental Health in Bethesda, Maryland, conducted research simulating the pre-industrial pattern of long nights of sleep. He had subjects spend fourteen hours in darkness every night for a month. Three weeks after the volunteers caught up on their seventeen hours of accumulated sleep debt (lost sleep from their everyday lives), they began a sleep pattern of about eight and a quarter hours per night, divided by two quiet rest states that resembled the brain wave patterns of meditation.

Wehr conjectures that "in prehistoric times this [sleep] arrangement provided a channel of communication between dreams and waking life that has gradually been closed off as humans have compressed and consolidated their sleep. If so, then this alteration might provide a physiological explanation for the observation that modern humans seem to have lost touch with the wellspring of myths and fantasies." [*The New York Times Magazine,* January 5, 1997]

We treat sleep like a project, expecting to sleep "a single, uninterrupted dose" that will not "get in the way of a busy schedule." We still dream but without the spaciousness that dreams need to enter our consciousness.

We may not be able to sleep for as long as our ancestors did before the advent of electricity, but we can view our sleep patterns in new ways. For instance, if you tend to wake during the night, allow yourself to drift in and out of the semi-awake state. This "nonproductive" state allows your consciousness to connect with its source. If you want to know your inner life more intimately, make sure that you get enough sleep. When you are awake, give yourself the spaciousness to gather and learn from your dreams.

Creating a Spacious Cave

Once you have paid proper attention to your sleep pattern, you can create a symbolic cave to sleep in. What does the physical space around your bed look like? Is there room beside your bed? What is your process in going to sleep at night? Do you crowd your night with activity? Do you go to bed willingly or reluctantly? Do you drink alcohol or take a sleeping pill?

Space is essential. Your room need not be large, but you should make room to support your intention. Clear the papers and books off your bed table and make room for a journal and pen. You are now ready to receive your dreams. As I write this, my bedroom bookcase overflows onto the floor; my nightstand, however, is not cluttered. Next to my bed is my dream journal with a pen inside at a blank page, awaiting a new dream.

Intention for Gathering

After creating space by your bed and placing your dream journal within reach, make an affirmation to yourself. Just before sleep tell yourself that you will remember and record your dreams. These are acts of intention.

The unconscious responds to training and habit. Writers learn that if they sit down to write at the same time each day, their inspiration gets accustomed to showing up at that time. Dreams, too, are vehicles for messages from the unconscious, so you should prepare for them in an organized and intentional fashion. While dreams seem incredibly spontaneous, capturing them requires focus. If we work randomly with our dreams, we lose their steady guidance.

As you lie down to sleep, listen quietly and state your desire regarding your dreams that night. It may be as simple as "I wish to remember my dreams" or "I will write down the dreams that come to me tonight." Or you may wish to ask for a dream to help you understand something that troubles you. You may ask to be awake, to be present, within your dreams. This quiet moment helps create a valuable psychic space in which your dreams can commune with you.

Keeping a Journal

When you awaken, write down or record your dream. Later, when you have time, you can re-enter the dream space and begin to communicate with it. The simplest way to catch your dreams is to record them, as soon as possible, on paper or with a tape recorder.

I prefer a journal; I don't want to waken my mate, and I enjoy physically putting words on paper to capture my dreams in the moment. Even if my nighttime jottings are sloppy, I do not have to transcribe a tape recording the next morning; I can immediately work with my dream. As soon as possible I jot down what is going on in my life, dialogue with a dream character, or simply highlight key phrases.

It doesn't matter how you choose to record dreams. What is important is capturing the dream's details and atmosphere before the dream fades. An hour after the dream, you will have lost many of the quirky, evocative details that can lead you to its hidden meaning.

Record the dream when you receive it, as close to the dreaming state as possible even if this means interrupting your sleep. Write your dream before your waking mind has taken hold; you will find that you record amazing little details or twists that your rational self would ignore when it takes charge after you're fully awake.

As you collect dreams over a long period of time, repeated images and details will reveal your particular inner landscape. If you dream frequently of ice and snow, you can explore the sense of coldness in or around you. Begin with your associations to coldness. Perhaps coldness reminds you of your unemotional grandmother, or of a parent who acted coldly whenever the two of you disagreed, or when you expressed a strong desire of your own. Perhaps coldness reminds you of solitude or independence—of someone who you know who built a fishing hut every winter on a frozen lake. As you gather these details, think about what memories and feelings they evoke in you and record them in your journal.

Our dreams have messages of wisdom for us. These messages

will recur if we can't hear the truth when it is first expressed; we are slow to open to the need for change. The better we listen, the clearer we become. Dreams come through us; we are the channels. Where we are clear, so are they. Where we are distorted, the messages may be hidden in puns, in bizarre settings, or they may be spoken by a dream character we don't like, have forgotten, or idealize.

Initial Exploration

You can begin your exploration with some quick steps that will reveal a lot about the dream's meaning for you. Do these before you ask someone else what he or she thinks the dream means. The dream is yours. Trust that it will guide you to answers, and that these initial steps will initiate understanding. It is important that you feel connected to your dream before others touch it.

- Date the dream

    It is essential to date each dream to place it into the context of your life.

- Title each dream

    This one is easy. Quickly place an intuitive title at the top of each dream. This will help you synthesize and remember it. It will also help you sort your dreams. It may reveal something crucial and elusive.

- Write initial impressions

    Jot down some initial impressions about the dream's meaning.

- Highlight Key Phrases

    Highlight phrases that stand out for you. They help you locate the heart of the dream. You can use these phrases later in your creative dream play. When reviewing a group of dreams, highlighted phrases often trigger connections or themes with other dreams.

Here are some examples from my dream journal.

Title: *How I Juice Myself Up*

Dream: *I have an amazing car. As long as I keep giving it juice, it keeps leaping up the steep mountain bank. It makes an enormous leap into the air and over the top where the video store is. I am afraid and aware of the incredible energy the car has in bucking and belting up the cliff.*

Thoughts: This dream tells me I am *driving* myself again, revving up my energy. I'm lured by the amazing energy I can mobilize. However, to keep driving in this way requires me to continually *juice up* myself. The underlying truth in this dream: Do I really need to be climbing cliffs? My energy really needs to be calmed instead of juiced.

Title: *Grandfather's Prayer Ritual*

Dream: *My grandfather, who is not born to Hebrew prayers and ritual, adopts them for himself, saying them every day, davening in his own Germanic way, wearing the burgundy and white striped shirt I gave him.*

Thoughts: This dream speaks of my strong connection to Judaism and its rituals even though I was not born to Judaism. It is my heart saying I can express my love for Judaism in my own creative way.

In-Depth Exploration

> ... have patience with everything unresolved in your heart and try to love the questions themselves as if they were locked rooms or books written in a very foreign language ... Live the questions now. Perhaps then, someday far in the future, you will gradually, without even noticing it, live your way into the answer.
>
> —Rainer Maria Rilke
> *Translated by Stephen Mitchell*

Listen to the dream's questions

Dreams pose compelling questions if we decide to hear them. Reread your dream and try to understand what it is asking of you. Sometimes it is asking a very clear question, which you may be ready to answer. Other times you may feel stumped and want to ask the dream a question. The answers may come rapidly or, as Rilke says, you may need to live with the questions until you discover you are living the answers.

There are times when I feel vaguely uncomfortable upon waking, as if I am not rested. The dream I have just had doesn't seem to have anything to do with this awful feeling. For example, one morning I woke up feeling very cold. I wanted to stay in bed all day. I wrote down what I could remember from my last dream and drifted off to sleep again. When I awoke a few minutes later, my feelings had sharpened. Now, instead of vague discomfort, I felt a clear sorrow, an old sadness. An unglamorous, plotless dream had dropped me into feeling what it is like to be completely unseen, a ghost among those who say they love you.

The Dream: *I have returned to college, to the beginning, why I don't know because I already have a master's degree. But here I am, bogged down by family responsibilities. I've been sick, and I don't like these courses, especially the science one. I am failing. I have a big bag of rocks I must identify and the book doesn't cover rocks. I decide to withdraw from school. I don't want Ds and Fs on my record. I don't like to quit, but I can't do this anymore. When I tell my husband, he looks at me as if I am invisible. When I insist that he hear me, he is critical of my decision, totally unsupportive. I am bereft. I am all alone again. I feel broken.*

All my life I have run from this cold, broken feeling when others do not see me. I ask myself, "Who needs another college degree?" Suddenly I know this question is the title of my dream. If I can answer it honestly, I will no longer be invisible to myself.

Understand That Each Character and Object in the Dream is an Aspect of You

In dreams you may appear as an observer or a participant. It is easy to identify yourself, but what are all these other people, animals or objects doing in your dream? Don't confuse yourself and think that because you are dreaming about others that the dream is a literal message about that person. These other dream characters and objects reflect aspects of you. In the above dream, my husband does not see me. This implies that I may not be seeing myself clearly.

2. RECEIVING AND GATHERING DREAMS

Understanding this helps me to continue exploring what the dream is asking of me. Do I disregard my real needs and demand that I keep *doing*? Isn't *being* more valuable than a meaningless, extra degree? I think of how unseen I was in my childhood. As my heart opens to those old feelings of invisibility, I actually begin to relax. I feel relieved of the relentless burden of continual accomplishment in a fruitless drive to be recognized.

Keep a Daily Review

Write a brief description of your day, not the activities but your feelings, the quality of your relationships, your issues and concerns, and any significant events that happened to you.

A dream may repeat the events of your day. This helps us process the residue of our waking world and anchor us in the reality of our lives. If your dream repeats a shocking event in a different context, it may release your shock. If the content of your dream does not seem to come from your daily life, your soul may be addressing deeper issues in your life. Comparing your dreams with your daily life can show you where your inner work lies. If your outer world is relatively calm and your dream life is disturbing, your soul may be saying it is time to heal some hidden conflicts or distortions. If your dreams are calm and your daily life is in turmoil, there may be undiscovered resources being revealed in your dreams that you can call on, such as a strength or an attribute you haven't tapped. The division between dreams and daily life is not always obvious. In either case you may ask, "Why am I not living what my dreams are showing me? Why am I not healing what my dreams are showing me?"

One recent night, I had two dreams. One cleared up residue from the previous day, underscoring what I already knew. The other dream invited me to explore it further. Until I looked at each dream closely, I didn't know what I was receiving.

Before the dreams I had reviewed, in writing, the events of the day.

"I'm frustrated with living for years in the small spaces of my house. I'm pushing for expansion—either building a new garage with a large room above it or buying a new house. Our friends are buying. I really want to live close to them. I know we are making a financial commitment to the girls' education, and my time is committed to my writing. Moving or building now would be a strain. My mind says "Stay small." My feelings are screaming, "It's enough!"

Then I had two dreams. At first I thought I they were meaningless, but as I wrote them, I knew they were messages from my soul.

1. *A woman struggled for years to earn a living. She says to me, "It's hard out there." She is always living poorly.* I title this dream "Living Poorly."
2. *Michael and I take the girls to an entertainment center. The girls remember the restaurants from our previous visit. They each pick their favorite place to eat, but their choices are expensive. Then Michael and I notice a small cafeteria. I decide it will do fine. I don't want to spend so much money or split up the family, Michael going with one girl and me with the other. The girls will be mad. But it's time to rein in the spending.* Of course, I title this dream, "Rein in the Spending."

Both dreams seem clear, yet as I title them, I realize the first dream is not as clear as the second. I initially think the first dream is warning me: If I expand too much, I'll end up poor. But that's not really what this dream is saying. I remember saying to myself as I watched the woman in the dream, "I wonder why she finds it so hard out there. I don't feel the same way." I imagine her. I see how she stands against the wind. She reminds me of my destitute aunt, whose chest was gaunt and fingers were stained with nicotine. I need to explore this. I will dialogue with my aunt and paint her. Her beliefs live hidden inside me, but I have always pushed them away by expanding my environment. I realize this is not the time to be building or moving. Staying in my small, perfectly lovely house will allow me to explore my inner poverty and sorrow. I want my expansion to be an organic development, not an escape from hidden, unbearable feelings. When it is time to expand, I don't want my destitute self to haunt the new space.

Trust your feelings and intuition

You have examined your day. Now it is time to trust your intuition. Does a dream keep nudging at you? When you are quiet, which dream appears? Do you have a strong feeling about a particular dream? Are you drawn to one character? Do you dislike a dream, or a character in it?

Pay attention to the voice that whispers, "Take a look at this dream." And don't worry whether you have chosen the "right" dream. Any dream can be mined for treasures that will help you.

Resolving Roadblocks to a Fluid Dream Life

Until one is committed, there is hesitancy, the chance to turn back. Concerning all acts of initiation (and creation) there is one elementary truth, the ignorance of which kills countless ideas and splendid plans. That the moment one definitely commits oneself, then Providence moves, too.

—Goethe

Sometimes our dreams appear as fragments. They may be incomplete or hazy, or we may not remember them. We feel discouraged that we haven't captured their meanings. But every facet of the dream experience is valuable, no matter how insignificant or inconsequential it seems.

We all face resistance to the dream process. Resistance is really fear—fear of the unknown, fear of uncovering what is hidden, fear of change. We may not recognize resistance: it is often indirect. We think, "That wasn't a very important dream." "I can only remember a fragment. That won't help." "How silly." "How stupid." "I'm so tired. I'll write it later." "Why bother? I'll never understand it, anyway."

After nearly thirty years of recording my dreams, I still encounter arguments when I first awaken with a dream. An internal voice might say, "This is an unimportant dream, really boring and unimaginative. Forget it." I have learned not to trust this voice. I have learned to record my dreams, regardless of the arguments, and make decisions about their value later. The moment of awakening from sleep is not the best time for evaluation. Challenge the voice of resistance and forge ahead, recording and working with whatever dream comes to you.

2. RECEIVING AND GATHERING DREAMS

Dream Fragments

Often you can catch only a fragment of a dream; the rest slips rapidly away. This dream shadow lingers, while the whole dream hangs in eclipse on the other side of the moon. The dream was fully visible in your sleep a moment ago. What can you do with your frustration? What can you do with fragments? Are they important?

Actually, fragments are simpler to work with than long, complicated dreams. They cut right to the point. They are easier to hold in your consciousness. They illuminate an individual's process. A fragment may be the missing link in a series of dreams. When you slip it into a sequence, you can see the pattern that was already present more clearly.

I dreamed *of a page of my manuscript. The manuscript is bound and ready to have the cover put on. The stitching is invisible and the spine is held up by a guy wire. This manuscript page is the obituary page.* I awoke thinking of "loosening the strict bonds that keep me unfinished." This dream reminded me that my old tight self is dying. I'm naked, like the octopus without a skin, awaiting a new cover. I wonder why I need a "guy" to hold me together. In the past a guy and harem clothes held the octopus together. I have grown out of that phase, and I am ready to wear my new skin.

Emotions evoked by even the smallest piece of a dream can lead you to richer insights. Only the dreamer's imagination can discover what the fragment has to say. When I began Kabbalistic healing studies, I had a dream fragment that a red dog had adopted me. The dog was like a golden retriever that had belonged to a friend. But when I recorded the dream, I wrote "a red German shepherd." This mistake sparked my interest so I contemplated this dream image of a red dog adopting me, and I soon began to cry. For some reason I was deeply comforted that this dog would want to be my companion.

As I let him comfort me, I wondered why I wrote German shepherd for golden retriever. I associate retrievers, not German shepherds, with emotional warmth. My friend's retriever was named Shanti, meaning peace. The dog in my dream was a combination of a peaceful golden retriever and a German shepherd. As I began to focus on the word shepherd, I thought of *Psalms 23*. Crying, I read,

> Yahweh is my shepherd
> I lack for nothing.
> In meadows of green grass he lets me lie.
> To the waters of repose he leads me;
> there he revives my soul.
>
> —*Psalms 23:1-3, The Jerusalem Bible*

I still don't understand why this dream moved me so, but I felt comforted by this dog who could lead me to my deepest rest where my soul could be revived. The dream also led me to explore my associations with "German." I thought of my dream of "Grandfather's Prayer Ritual," where my Germanic grandfather adopts a Jewish prayer ritual. I imagined a retriever/shepherd helping me to retrieve part of my lost spiritual heritage. As I worked with this dream, I sensed my soul confirming the rightness of my Kabbalistic studies. I looked at my associations to the dog's colors, both red and golden: red the color of passion, my Gram's penchant for red, the fire of my inner life; gold, the color of the sun, light, riches, the wealth of the self. This work affirmed my retrieval of my own rich, passionate self. For days this dream dog seemed present, accompanying me through life.

Forgotten Dreams

If you cannot remember your dreams, a creative practice will help to enhance your dream recall. For example, write in your journal the moment you awaken, before you start your day. Write three or four pages, with no purpose other than allowing your hidden thoughts and feelings to emerge. Follow the ideas freely as they skip around, or as one idea triggers another. When you stop, ask yourself if you have come to the natural end of this associative process. You may have stopped because you were resistant to staying open. When you are satisfied that you have come to the end of your writing, let go of this material, trusting that a door has been opened to your unconscious. Perhaps your dream or its energy and truth will come through that door. If not, continue this practice every morning, before you become engaged with the day and your waking mind takes over.

You can draw what you are feeling when you awaken. Keep an unlined dream journal along with crayons, markers, or colored pencils by your bed. If you do not have any images to draw, draw the colors of how you feel. Make abstract shapes. Or draw a circle and fill it with the colors you intuitively select. Let the circle be your self. Let the act of filling it be your soul's expression.

Dreams have their own laws and logic. Through experimentation, you can enhance your dream recall. They come to your consciousness when you call out to them in their creative expression.

Incomplete Dreams

Some dreams are unfinished. The dream may end abruptly or an alarm or a loud sound may interrupt it. You can often finish the dream either by returning to sleep or by reentering the dream with your imagination.

John's dreams tell him stories. If the story is incomplete, he finishes it. John describes how he completed a recent dream. "While I was sick with the flu, I had the most wonderful dreams, like a continuous walk through my semi-conscious. One of those dreams I called 'Climbing.' To me it was the classic hero's voyage.

"A group of us are climbing up a snow-covered mountainside. It's barren, no vegetation. Just rocks. We are not far from the summit. This mountain is a huge bunch of rubble. As we approach the summit, the group recognizes that we have left behind something very, very important. So we get together and talk about what we should do. It is vital that we have this. I volunteer, along with two others to go back down the mountain to get IT. We start off, and part way down we fall through a hole at the roots of a tree stump. I fall down, not too far, into a world of desolation, an urban area that has been virtually destroyed, a post-atom bomb environment. Fires are burning everywhere. The sky is blotted out with dirt. Yellow-red clouds hover over this city. We land in a basketball court. We set about looking for IT. I start going through the rubble. I assume we are the only survivors in this holocaust-type environment. There are gangs preying on survivors. Suddenly a gang of young males

comes to attack us. We run. They catch up to us and we fight. We are victorious and manage to beat off these thugs. After the battle I am alone. I don't know where my companions are."

John woke up from this dream and knew immediately it was the quintessential hero's journey. He says, "It gives me a great amount of pleasure to associate with that imagery. It reminds me of the Bodhisattva on the road to enlightenment. Climbing up the mountain is symbolic of this. There is the remembrance of some part of me left behind, and my volunteering to return so I can bring it back for the collective good. The place we returned to turns out to be rubble and death. I want to associate with the hero who does this.

"But the dream was unfinished for me. So I closed my eyes and went back. *Suddenly I found myself on the mountainside in clear, cold sunlight, climbing back up.* Climbing back on the path finished the dream. I knew I had been to the underworld. I had defeated the devil or the beast that lives in the underworld, and in doing this, I was automatically transported back onto the path. I had been given a task to complete.

"Now I know a different world. Once I woke up and could touch the outside world, I could go back into the voyage to complete some work. This dream felt like my asking God for a sign that I am on the right path."

Flood of Dreams

Some dreamers are flooded by dreams. Perhaps this happens because the soul is always eager to reach the person's awareness. If this is the case, choose to record only one dream a night. Don't worry about which dream to choose. Soon your dream state will adjust and give you a manageable amount of dreams.

The dream state is like mother's milk, which contains everything the baby needs to grow. The mother is in constant attunement to the baby. At the beginning the mother usually produces more milk than the baby needs. After a few days of nursing, the breasts adjust their production to the baby's real needs. When the baby goes through a growth spurt and needs more milk, the breasts will increase their flow within a few days. Our souls are like mothers in this way. The soul adjusts the flow of dreams to our needs when we communicate these needs to the soul.

2. RECEIVING AND GATHERING DREAMS

A Conscious Dreamer: Alice

Alice was a member of a woman's dream circle that I ran for several years. She is an artist who graces her whole life with the symbols of her interior world. She is attentive to the messages and symbols that come to her through her dreams and imaginal voyages, from her waking life, and from others' dreams. Whatever touches her she honors in her art. In a real way, Alice lives art. There is little distinction for her between the symbolic events of her waking life and her nightly dreams. All she creates and re-creates is done simply, quietly, and consistently. Underlying her creativity is her regular recording of her dreams.

"I keep a journal of my life. I write down my dreams in this journal. I make small pictures of the symbols from my dreams and from things that happen around me—subtle things that mean something to me. Many times I include words and phrases or quotes with these. Then I make a book of the year. It's my spiritual book. Sometimes it's not so spiritual. Part of it I write in code. For example, the year I had a breast removed, I didn't put that in, only the symbols around it like the bed my husband made for us that year.

"After the year is over and I've put together the book, I reread it and break it down and see what part of it comes from my dreams, or my family, my Christ group, my reading, walking, painting, or my husband and friends, the dream girls, the paint girls, my vacations, or other activities. That's when I know what is important to me. I can see what things make me go 'Wow,' and which ones bring tears.

"It's been very important to me to make this yearly book. It gives me strength to have the knowledge of what is important to me. It makes it more real. I bind this book and title it. For me it's a synthesis of what is significant to me. I have an ordinary life, but it's a wonderful life."

Alice did not always connect to metaphor and symbol. She worked at her first career, writing for an advertising trade publication in New York City, until she married at age twenty-eight. When her children were in grade school, she was part of an avant-garde performing group that traveled in Europe for a month at a time. Later she was active in the art world in New York.

Now in her 70's, Alice loves her symbols and her love pours out in whimsical, unexpected creations. She often appears in dream group with a new inspiration. Once she brought a bound book made from a child's book-making kit. Another time she brought cards she had created from her dream symbols, so we could select individual cards related to our dreams. She gave us reproductions of her paintings of dream horses, computer-scanned from her original watercolors. She made plates with paintings of her symbols, using children's plate-making kits. One was of "two lovers, crow and wolf, and the moon and the stars."

Most recently, Alice has been making totems. One totem clearly illustrates the process Alice uses in allowing an image to work through her. It is "Porcus Dei," a divine pig which she relates to the Agnus Dei, or Lamb of God. Alice says, "Porcus Dei" is a way of saying everything is God's.

"My work with my symbols comes about in a complicated way. Once I was traveling in Italy and was very taken with a sculpture in a

2. RECEIVING AND GATHERING DREAMS

church of Agnus Dei. I took a photo of it. Much later this symbol came up from my subconscious during an imaginal journey in a group. It came out as a pig, a common animal, in a boat carrying a cross. I made a little drawing of it. I didn't expect anything more. But later I began thinking of it. I wanted to make something I could feel. I was in the process of making a few totems from old journals, all my old dream drawings, a lot of notes over the years, and a lot of clippings I've saved. I put the papers into hot water and then rolled them with a rolling pin, put some glue on them and made totems, which I hung on the wall in my room.

"All my dream group notes went into one totem of a sleeping woman. I included a rose pinecone from France, which Raechel gave to each of us. When we had a dream group at a garden, I made a wreath of the dried grass during lunch. I put it into a totem along with the take-outs of a book I made this year. Another totem is crowned with tall crow's feathers. It has a nest in the middle and a piece of glass in it, all gathered from my walks.

"Porcus Dei appeared in a renewal imaginal journey in Raechel's group to start the New Year. In the center of the room on a mirror was a bowl of water. To me things like this bowl of water and Porcus Dei are more real than a lot of the art I've been doing over the years. They feel more authentic. They have a lot of substance behind them."

Alice's relationship to her symbols is as personal as her dreams. Her connection to imagery goes beyond her dreams; it touches and connects all her life experiences. Alice holds her life both lightly and seriously.

"One night I dreamed I was looking up at the sky. There in the sky was a word of seven letters, but I couldn't remember what the letters were when I woke up. I knew there were a lot of vowels in it. I started to think about the dream and it came out ENDOMAI.

"I didn't know what it meant so I shared it in our dream group. Raechel suggested doing a mandala every day for seven days and letting the mandalas tell me its meaning. I liked that idea, but instead of mandalas, I did a small painting every day, staying with the letters. I quietly waited to see if anything came. One day I knew. It means God in me. I stopped waiting. That week of paintings became the foundation for a little book about ENDOMAI, called *The Cow and the Sea*. The inspiration was a cow I saw in the Metropolitan Museum of Art. This mythical, mysterious animal was carrying a container that was a gift. I identify with the cow. I think we give each other gifts.

"All the images that went into this book came from my dreams or someone else's, like the double-yolked eggs shared by another dreamer. The sea that I painted came from one of my dreams that had a marble palace with columns and a frothy, blue sea. In the book, I had the cow coming up out of this sea.

"Endomai is one of my words now. After you share a creative symbol or dream, it becomes a part of your lexicon. It's not hidden, and it can be used. There are times, though, when I only share the symbol, and I don't say what I think it means because it means too much to me. I have a tremendous amount of trust. I feel everything is all right, basically. I bring that trust to my dream work."

2. RECEIVING AND GATHERING DREAMS

The Cow and the Sea

The cow came up out of the crystal sea, carrying something in her arms.

It smelled like hard rain . . .

but it may have been a magic hat, or double-yolked eggs.

One night, a very big storm came to the field, and she was afraid, but she stayed in the white call of the geese until she fell asleep.

She dreamed she was a green package whose head needed to be held softly.

And woke up singing an Italian love song.

Then she had her nails done at the Excelsior and went to find her love.

On the way, she saw a truck with fires on it

and some wings with white circles on them

and a word in the sky, ENDOMAI.

And that is what she was bringing up out of the sea in her arms.

This time, anyway.

3

Creating a Spiritual Practice

> The images that arise from your depths transform your consciousness. They move forward your inner intention to nourish yourself. They help repair or heal the world. They turn past the boundaries of the old, rigidified self. They move you into the possibility of your own becoming.
>
> —Judith Schmidt

What is a Spiritual Dream Practice?

Without a conscious effort to understand and learn from a dream, it easily slips away or remains a fantasy. A dream practice helps you be in relationship to your dream. It is a choice to connect the invisible and visible worlds. A practice arises directly from your dream. It is a repetitive action which you create to make a conscious bridge between your outer, waking life and the hidden realm of spirit. You might approach it as a personal ritual.

A dream practice keeps the dream alive. At the same time it solidifies the dream's wisdom and leads to the fulfillment of your intention.

A dream practice is a holy act, born from your soul. It is not imposed on you from the outside. It is a gift from the quiet voice inside you, which works invisibly. This practice makes real changes possible. It can help you become happier, wiser, more empathic, calmer, or more capable.

Each unique practice is born from a specific dream or imaginal journey. Listen to your own dream for guidance rather than rely on a list of set practices. Let yourself be creative. Your practice can be as unusual and varied as your dreams: reciting a mantra, walking daily in the woods, eating a special food consciously, visiting the dream every day, or drawing a mandala on a dream theme.

The Dream's Transformative Power

A practice can be very simple. A woman who dreams she is in a cave with a polished dome and stars on the ceiling decides to sit in this cave every day, waiting to see what she would like to do there. She might feel like dancing or painting herself.

One of my simplest practices came out of a dream about the actress and director Jodie Foster. *She is locked up behind immense stacks of boxes in a warehouse, hiding from a disturbed young man who wants to possess her. The villagers hear her running back and forth, wildly crashing into the boxes. For weeks, she tries to claw her way out of her self-created prison. She can no longer bear to be separated from others, yet no one comes to her rescue. She finally escapes and runs screaming into the civilized village. After she escapes, she hides by becoming unreal.*

I re-entered this dream and knew immediately that I was hiding in fear of my real self. Afterwards I did a simple visual practice, called

"Jodie's Boxes." Each day I drew in my journal a box containing a situation that was currently *boxing* me in. When I finished doing this practice, I saw how easily I build walls that keep me from surrendering to my heart. Most of the boxes began with a verb. They were all acts of *doing*: painting sets and fretting over the chaos around the show, drinking another cup of tea, cleaning out the attic, putting others' needs first, rereading all of my dreams to get a handle on my imagery—anything to avoid sitting alone with a candle and music. This practice kept the dream alive for me and showed me how I have used my energy destructively. It helped me to transform my compulsive activity to *being* and *doing* calmly.

A practice can be silent, without words or art. One of my practices was to sense a coiled, still snake at the base of my spine. This practice originated with a dream in which *I lose track of my pet snake, Ananta, and then find her being attacked by my male cat who was obsessed with this ice cold, bleeding snake. I rescue Ananta but become sidetracked* (a common occurrence with me). *When I remember her and return to get her, she lunges at me. She is crazed that I have forgotten her.*

I awoke in terror, knowing this dream must be addressed.

The first thing I took note of was my snake's name Ananta, named for the great Hindu serpent symbol of the Infinite. Immediately, I knew that once again I had become sidetracked from the most essential part of my life. I had become too caught up in *doing* and had forsaken a heart connection to the Infinite.

Dr. Neil Russack, a Jungian analyst and author of *Animal Guides*, says that meeting a snake "is one of the great goals of the inner journey" but we are often shocked by the encounter. "When we meet the snake, the shock of that meeting poses a question for us." Shocked by my snake, I knew this was an important dream, asking me to live a radically different way. It was time for me to create a practice of remembering. I first explored the dream in a literal way. I took my pet snake Ananta from her cage; she glided inside the bathrobe I was wearing and curled up at the base of my spine. I soon felt calm and centered. After that, whenever I began to feel possessed by my *doing*, I would imagine the snake curling against my spine and my tension would dissolve. This became my practice for the next two weeks.

This is a wordless practice. I tried to add a daily exercise of conversing with the snake, but it was dissatisfying. With this dream it felt forced and unnatural to work with words. As James Hillman says, "The moment you've caught the snake in an interpretation, you've lost the snake."

Clearly, the Infinite wants my presence in an embodied, non-mental way. I am being propelled toward a deeper spiritual life. This silent, tactile knowing heals my way of being. It's a step in the direction of living consciously in the Infinite, and will eventually lead me to a spiritual practice called Impersonal Movement™ (taught by A Society of Souls).

The dream has potential to change us, if we take action. When we don't act on the dream, the transformative power of the dream is diluted. The dream can easily remain a fantasy, an escape from life. A spiritual practice works invisibly as it grounds the imagination and continues the work of the dream.

A dream practice strengthens the intuition. Our ability to hear and act on our inner voice is often dulled during the school years, when the focus is on thinking. Until my late 40s I was convinced I had no intuitive ability. But years of dream practices opened my intuitive and emotional functions, which I now consider my principal strengths.

The Seven Sleepers Teaching

The long sleep of the Seven Sleepers was an act of spiritual practice. These dreamers knew the significance of remembering a dream through practice, according to the custom of their people.

I imagine that before the Sleepers entered the cave, each had a dream of his own—variations on the same dream—the seemingly impossible task of dreaming the world whole.

In that time before their stay in the cave, they began their daily practices living apart from one another. One prayed for a dream for someone in need. Another painted the cross in every possible form. The third dreamer visualized herself dreaming and being awake at the same time. Each day, the fourth meditated on the previous night's dream. The next dreamer bathed consciously, imagining himself being cleansed of negativity. One sang a song of thanksgiving for the changes in the world, as if they had already taken place. The last dreamer gathered a stone each day, painting it with the symbols that had appeared in her dream.

For twenty-one days, each dreamer did a spiritual practice directly related to his or her dream. After twenty-one days of practice, they rested for seven days. When the Emperor ordered the dreamers into the cave, they surrendered to a long sleep. As they slept, the Seven Sleepers continued to practice the art of dreaming. Dream by dream they helped heal the world, uniting the fragments of consciousness until all individuals could know compassion within themselves and experience their connection with one another.

When we enter the cave with the Sleepers, we become aware of the process of transformation. At first, like us, they are awake only between dreams. At those times they renew their commitment to their practice. As years pass, the dreamers evolve until they are awake within their dreams. Eventually their life of waking, sleeping, and dreaming becomes a seamless whole, where commitment is taken with each breath, and there is no distinction between practice and the dream. They are living in harmony with their souls. They are ready to die from this world. Yet they continue to dream on, until the people in the outside world are the living embodiment of the Seven Sleepers' spiritual practices. The Sleepers have completed their task and can leave the cave to return home.

Fundamentals of a Ritual Practice

> My visits to Clarity are soothing now. I still remember the first time I went to see him ... He lives on a hill in a little house surrounded by wild roses. I went in the living room and sat down in a comfortable chair by the fireplace. There were topographical maps on the walls, and the room was full of stuff, musical instruments and telescopes and globes, geodes and crystals and old Italian tarot decks, two small

cats. When I left, he presented me with a sketchbook and told me to draw the same thing every day until the drawing started to speak to me.

—J. Ruth Gendler

One of the originators of spiritual dream practice is Madame Colette Muscat of Jerusalem. She has been teaching the art of waking dream and imaginal journeys for many years. These fundamentals come from her teachings, passed on by her students.

- Always let the dream imagery inspire your ritual practice.
- Remember that anything can be a practice, as long as it is done with consciousness and commitment to your own growth.
- Only a short amount of time is necessary each day for a dream practice. An appropriate practice does not require a huge time commitment. It only requires that you honor the gift of your dream.
- As you practice, the dream imagery works on the unseen within you. It will evolve as you continue to dream and work with your dreams. Your imagery will eventually form a seamless whole, despite the chaotic mix of images and stories in your dreams.
- Know that selecting and doing a practice strengthens your intuition.
- Renew your commitment to your practice every day for seven or twenty-one days. These periods have a mystical energy and add power to the practice.
- After a cycle of twenty-one days, rest for seven days to allow you time to assimilate the changes you have initiated.

- If you want to continue this particular practice, renew it for another seven or twenty-one days. Or choose another, related to your dream.

How to Create a Practice

1. Select a recent dream that is important to you. If you have extended the dream through writing or art, include these.
2. Reread the dream. Sit quietly with your imagery, perhaps lighting a candle or incense first. Listen to the message of the dream, as you know it now.
3. Imagine the ways you could carry the gift of this dream into your waking life. Be playful and creative. Remember to let the dream imagery inspire you.
4. Choose a practice that you can see yourself doing. Do not agonize over your choice. Just trust yourself. It will come to you. There is no right or wrong practice.

Working With Resistance

We use our ego or thought process to decide on a dream practice. From that moment the ego may resist, at first aggressively, later on more subtly. You will quickly learn the ways you resist change. Here are a few forms of resistance I encounter regularly.

Judgment

Judgment arises as criticism, such as: "How can this make a difference in my life? I have to fix things. This practice is simplistic; bizarre; impossible; it's magical thinking." Behind judgments usually lie feelings of need and vulnerability. Try to suspend your judgment. Do the practice with an open mind like a researcher. If you let the criticisms go, there will be space for the deeper "I" to bring about change. There will be room for the unknown and the impossible to occur. A tight mind hinders transformation.

Forgetting

If you forget or put off your practice, sit quietly and ask yourself why you have lost your eros for this practice. Then ask yourself if this is the best practice for this dream. Is this the best practice for you at this time? Is this dream nudging at deeper material that you have not touched yet? The answers to these questions will help you resume your practice or find another one. You may also need to ask two more questions. Does this practice need to evolve in a different direction? Can you let the practice change?

A practice does not need to be static. It is important to give it space just as a seedling needs air and loose earth around it to send out shoots and roots. Before you plant a seed, you often add humus to aerate the soil. When you do a practice, you need to include emotional, mental, and psychic humus.

If you continually forget to do your practice, ask yourself what you are feeling. Are you judging or punishing yourself for your lack of action? Are you afraid that you won't be successful? Being critical will not improve your practice. Your practice and your dream will keep working even when you are trying to stop it. Your soul wants the best for you and will continue to creatively assist you. Just do your practice as often as you can and empathize with your struggle.

A practice can be difficult to sustain because you may not understand what the practice means until you have done it. A dream has many levels of meaning, which may become clearer over the years. A practice evolves out of the same mystery. Ritual reveals its meaning in time. Until it does, you must trust the practice. The dream originates in a non-logical place where trust and faith arise. Stay there. Knowing will follow.

Doubt

Sometimes people question whether their effort is paying off. Real and lasting change from within takes much longer than willed change. We tend to demand quick changes because we are in a hurry to alleviate our suffering. Lasting happiness is brought about less obviously. Dreamwork deals with intangible processes, which bring about real transformation. We must be willing to accept subtle changes before the big ones appear.

Pay careful attention to this subtle process and its results; what you are changing is a state of mind. It is possible to change and not even realize it. Or you may be living from a new state of mind and not be aware of how you arrived here.

Despair

It is more difficult to do a dream practice when you need it most. When you are feeling lost, it is hard to focus your attention on a practice. By summoning your active will, you will be more likely to find direction through your practice.

Trust in repetition; it has always been essential in soul work. Simple repetitive practices, like the rosary prayer or a mantra, soothe and anchor spiritual intention. Little by little, the new imagery penetrates the old blockages and becomes a part of you.

3. CREATING A SPIRITUAL PRACTICE

A Conscious Dreamer: Liz

Liz is a versatile artist who has written poetry and music, designed clothing, and created multi-dimensional art events. She is deeply and emotionally involved in her art and inner life. She is also a courageous dreamer who faces all of herself. Here she describes a pivotal dream, which led to a practice and new direction in her art.

"*I am driving along in a car. S. is driving. I'm beside her in front. J. is in the back, behind S. talking. I'm talking to S. Suddenly I realize that S. has been asleep for ages, and somehow the car has been driving itself. I'm totally amazed as I watch the car stay on its side of the road. The road is fairly straight, just a few ups and downs. Lots of trees and snow. I don't know if I tell J. that S. is asleep, but then I see that J. is leaning over the front with his hands on the wheel. We begin to speed up a hill, and I realize a train is coming and we are going to be hit. We are going faster and faster.*

"At this point in the dream, *when the train hits us, I know I am dreaming, but some part of me wants to know what death is like. I'm dead, or about to be dead; I'm in the process of dying. Time has become very strange, everything moving in slow motion with great clarity. I'm flying through the air, twisting and turning as if in a vast wind. The light is very bright. There seems to be a lot of color, mostly gold. I know I'm dying, and I'm trying to stay with the feelings and sensations, but am becoming more and more frightened. I don't want to die, and I begin to fight it. I am unable to watch or witness. I am in total reaction. I try to stay but I can't. I want out.* I wake up. Sweating. My heart pounding."

"When I had this dream, I had been fighting the part of me that wouldn't allow me to surrender, the part that wants things my way. I was often forcing things, but then I would feel like I was being crucified. Logically, I knew I needed to let go. I would pray about it, but I had so much terror about letting go. It seemed easier to stay with the excruciating pain. This part of the dream seemed obvious to me. My friend S. has a strong will, so it seemed that will was driving my life. Then J. took over the wheel. He's the part of me that uses being nice to get my way. My longing was to surrender to the dying. I knew that was what I should do, but there was no way I could."

Liz's practice came to her in a meditation. She was surprised when she saw a gold cross, big and heavy, smelling of well-crafted wood. She had a conversation with it.

Liz: Why have you come to me?

Cross: You keep asking why you are constantly being crucified. Why should the gateway to surrender be one of pain, suffering, shame, humiliation, and death?

Liz: Why is purification so painful?

Cross: Because you won't give up the fight. How can you shine like me when you are dirty? This purification is your bath, your cleansing.

Liz: Is there no other way?

Cross: You need to become who you really are. To strip away and stand naked. Through the gates you will strip away and become gold.

Liz: For me you are the symbol of the ultimate surrender, but why am I so afraid?

Cross: You need to surrender in small steps. Once I was a tree, tall and strong and straight, roots deep into Mother Earth. I would dance with the wind and bathe in the rain. Now I am a cross. But I am also a tree, transformed by a death.

"After this conversation, I decided spontaneously to do my practice with the cross. Logically, I would have expected to work with a gold light, or the snow and the road. Yet I could also see that the big piece for me in the dream was the terror of surrender, which explains the gift of the cross.

"I knew that without giving up my willfulness, I could not surrender into the gold. In fact, I realized from the dream that my will was tired and wanted to sleep, and the car was still on the road.

"I did my practice while I sat in meditation every day. Each day I would spend five to ten minutes envisioning the cross and see what came to me.

"At one point in the practice I saw a woman hanging from the cross, which I used in a major mixed media piece, called *For Sophia*. Using multi-media, I created this large work of art to honor the fourteen female victims of the Montreal massacre on December 6, 1989.

"When I began the piece, there was no willfulness involved. People just appeared to help me. I saw a woman at a concert who was so fused with gold that I asked her to pose for me. When I explained that this piece would hang upside down on the cross, she was shocked because she had been raped as a teenager. When she posed, she felt this was part of her healing of this rape.

"Also in my meditations on the golden cross, I would hear music and sound. When I approached a composer for permission to use his music, he agreed and even let me change some of the words. The singers volunteered their time. I have never done a piece with so many people and had such ease. Even the media quickly gave me permissions to use their broadcasts. It was an abundant experience.

"The piece was controversial and when it came to showing it, I was turned down twice. The first time I tried, it was with my will again. I pushed and pushed. It became a life and death issue, and I finally had to surrender that I could not control when it would be exhibited. A year after I completed the piece, it was shown in a gallery, along with a second piece that emerged out of my dream practice.

"This second piece is *My Stations of the Cross*. It came about because I realized that if I knew the steps along the way to surrendering, I wouldn't have to spend so much time on the cross. I could see what I was doing a little clearer.

"Just before the showing of *For Sophia*, the composer, who was also my friend, died in a car crash. As I mourned, I saw clearly when I was able to surrender to reality of his death and my grief, and when I fought it.

"I have learned so much from this dream and my practice with it. Both led me to about six pieces of artwork and seem to be the catalyst for the direction of my current art. All are about surrender and acceptance of myself, which then leads to acceptance of you and others.

"Growing up, I never knew any female way to be sacred. All the images were masculine. So this dream led to my knowing the female in a sacred way. When I did *For Sophia*, I had to nail her to the cross. I had always viewed myself as the victim, never the victimizer. I never realized that my forcing will is my victimizing part—the voice that is harsh, critical, pushing, demanding."

4

Transforming Dreams Into Creative Expressions

Turning-Point

For there is a boundary to looking.
And the world that is looked at so deeply
wants to flourish in love.

Work of the eyes is done, now
go and do heart-work
on all the images imprisoned within you; for you
overpowered them: but even now you don't know them.

—Rainer Maria Rilke
Translated by Stephen Mitchell

Speaking in Dream Language

Turning personal imagery into new forms unlocks their power and transforms the psyche. Choosing to explore your dreams creatively, you learn to communicate with them in their own language. If you traveled to France and did not know any French, you could enjoy the cities and landscapes and manage to get your basic needs met, but you would miss the nuances of French life—its heart and soul.

If you can speak the language of dreams, you have potential for deeper conversation and intimacy with them. Exploring the arts and trusting your imagination to inspire you, you enter the land where dream language is spoken. It is an endlessly creative language, composed of symbols and imagery. It is an artistic language, yet you do not have to be an artist to learn it. Many scientists and inventors have found answers and ideas in their dreams.

This is the playful part of dreamwork. All it requires is courage, a willingness to enter the creative void, and letting go of self-judgment. The purpose of this creative process is to honor and respect your dreams, to practice speaking their unique language, and to allow your creativity to act as the great healer it is.

The Seven Sleepers Teaching

When the Seven Sleepers recreate the world through their imagery, they enter the creative phase of the myth. The sleepers don't appear to be creating as they sleep for two hundred years. Their *doing* is trusting the dream and remaining in the dreaming state, creating new imagery. It requires an act of will to reenter the dream state imaginatively and to trust where the process leads.

In this imaginative phase we make the myth our own. This is where we re-enter our dreams to give them life and meaning. If we don't take this step, the dream remains outside us.

My curiosity made me wonder what this myth offered contemporary dreamers. My imagination fleshed it out. I imagine *that the Seven Sleepers are dreaming at a high level of creativity, so high they can link their imaginations into a single transformative dream.* All we see in the bare bones of the myth are seven young men or Sufi masters sleeping in a cave. We do not see their creation. Only when they emerge from their cave is their creation visible.

The creative process requires that we know when to step back, let go, and allow a deeper part of ourselves to act. Then new connections or adjustments to our creations can happen and we discover the soul of the work. As we give over to our deeper minds, it seems that nothing is happening. We may appear to sleep, but a great deal is occurring below the surface. Artists and writers understand the purpose of this seemingly empty state. Suddenly a new way of looking at a project arises, or a missing piece is found. We respond with an "aha!" We return to our artistry revitalized.

Reclaiming Your Hidden Language

Where is the child I was
still inside me or gone?

Does he know that I never loved him?
and that he never loved me?

Why did we spend so much time
growing up only to separate?

Why did we both not die
when my childhood died?

> And why does my skeleton pursue me
> if my soul has fallen away?
>
> —Pablo Neruda
> *Translated by William O'Daly*

We are born creative and begin our creative acts early. As children we learn quickly that parts of ourselves are unacceptable to our parents and the adults around us. We begin hiding these parts to protect ourselves. We can be so creative at hiding that, by the time we are adults, we no longer know that our real selves have disappeared. We live in some unreal, idealized way that doesn't match all of who we are. We may be outwardly successful at this endeavor, but inwardly we know something is missing.

"And why does my skeleton pursue me / if my soul has fallen away?" Pablo Neruda asks. Neruda's question strikes at the discomfort and the pressure I feel when I forget my real self.

For many of us, building a shield or false self around the real self was vital to our psychological survival as children. But as adults, living through a mask is a painful, unnecessary hindrance. It's false, inauthentic. It's like living in a beautiful mansion, isolated from our humanity. In order to grow spiritually, we must reconnect to the hidden essence that resides within the fortress we have created. How can we reclaim that true self when we have lost the language of the nonverbal child?

Children receive the world through their senses. As a child you

4. TRANSFORMING DREAMS INTO CREATIVE EXPRESSIONS

are sensitive to nuances—shadow or sunlight, fragrance or stench, the whisperings of mother's loneliness or her look of wonder when she gazes out of the corner of her eye at you, her creation. Without spoken language, the young child responds to the phenomenal world and communicates his emotional response, for example, gurgling delightfully over the way the shadow of a tree in sunlight dances across the wall, or fretting about a repetitive harsh sound. We believe we hear what others are saying; we don't realize that we are also listening to non-verbal cues at the same time. Yet we know that it requires openness, patience, experimentation, and intuitive listening to understand a baby. Many parents understand what their baby is trying to communicate, but they won't have any idea what their own personal inner child wants to communicate. This ability to sense the world and communicate with it seems to vanish as we become adults. Where did this non-verbal language go?

Most of us have never developed a language that can reach back and speak with that child we once were. There are four ways to connect with the extraordinary openness and sensitivity of the very young child: dream, reverie, imagination, and creative expression.

Dreams offer us access to the lost language of childhood. Conveyed in the language of the senses, dreaming is an excellent means of reclaiming what became hidden.

After dreaming, let yourself enter a state of reverie, opening to the dream's sensory imagery. This state of being is similar to the sensorial infant's attunement to the world. It expands the imagination, which the poet David Whyte describes as "an important felt sense central to our creative survival." In *The Natural Artistry of Dreams*, Jill Mellick tells us to circumambulate our dreams, letting "their images feed our imagination and lead us onward."

From the place of reverie, select a form of creative expression. Moving the dream into creative play, you are broadening and deepening this initial nighttime communication. Your artistic work will communicate aspects of your inner nonverbal reality. The combination of imagination and creativity will help to free you from the domination of a false self. It will help reconnect you with your essence. When you imbue the whole process with Spirit through prayerful intention, you reclaim your hidden language and heal the wound of separation from the child you once were.

Working With Resistance

Resistance toward creative expression reflects archetypal fears: fear of the unknown, fear of emptiness, fear of what will emerge. Judging ourselves is a way to hide our fears. Living from our imagination is the opposite of living from fear. Whereas fear freezes the soul, imagination invites the soul to dance and be fully alive. Here are some common judgments people have about creating from dreams:

"I'm not an artist or a writer." Most of us judge our attempts at making art, but even accomplished artists make rough sketches in preparation for a painting. Thinking of your dream artwork as a rough draft will help free your inhibitions.

Jeanne insists she can't draw faces. Yet after working on a dream

4. TRANSFORMING DREAMS INTO CREATIVE EXPRESSIONS

of an old woman, she spontaneously drew the woman's face. "It poured out of me," she said. She drew the woman's wispy gray hair, vivid blue eyes, and orange lips. In the picture the old woman looks "wise and mysterious, also a little scary and fierce." Jeanne is still startled when she looks at this painting of the "enigmatic old woman who knows the secrets of the universe, but doesn't give them away." When Jeanne sees this woman's face, she understands that one has to earn the secrets.

Imagine yourself making "dream expressive art" that is only for you to see. We are not training to become professional artists. We are "playing art" and getting acquainted with our soul language. We are giving the unconscious a form for its self-expression.

There are many ways to play with dreams. You can find in magazines pictures, words, and phrases that evoke the imagery in your dreams. Glue them onto paper, or into your dream journal. Or walk around with a camera and take photos, then make a collage by juxtaposing them into new relationships that evoke your dreams. All you need is a willingness to play and explore your inner world.

"My dreams are too ugly and painful." Often what lies between our real self and us is disturbing and painful. Our dreams can graphically reveal this. We need to know we can uncover our monsters and painful memories without being demolished by them. When we choose to be creatively involved with these parts, they no longer trap us. What has been hidden in the shadows of our unconscious comes out into the sunlight. The ironic part is that we think we are in control by suppressing the instinctual with our will and minds, when what is hidden actually has a stronger power over us. Until we expose what is concealed, we are in danger of being subverted by it. Seeing the enemy face-to-face is less threatening than dealing with a sniper.

Necessary Resistance

Working with dreams and the creative process can open up very powerful material. For some dreamers a certain kind of resistance will help slow down an out-of-control creative process that could detach a person from waking reality. It helps to remind yourself that this is only a dream designed to help you. Know the strength of your ego and your boundaries before you choose a creative dream technique. Pay attention to what happens when you enter the creative process. If you find yourself becoming ungrounded and forgetting your earthly responsibilities, slow down and seek someone trained to help integrate your dream material into your waking life—a counselor, therapist or teacher. You may need a more structured approach in order to explore your dreams and still function in your everyday reality. Can you pay your bills, get the laundry done, feed yourself, and still work with your dream life? If so, continue your creative exploration.

4. TRANSFORMING DREAMS INTO CREATIVE EXPRESSIONS

Creative Choices

Imagine inventing yellow or moving
For the first time in a cherry curve.

—M.C. Richards

Dreams lend themselves to any form of creative expression. You have a great many choices, and no one choice is more valuable than the others. Dreamers in my classes and workshops are surprisingly willing to try new possibilities. Their creations have taken many forms:

- a face painting
- a startling poem by a novice writer
- one image painted repeatedly, subtly changing as new imagery emerges from the psyche
- a spontaneous song accompanied by drums
- old dream drawings torn and transformed into a collage
- the diary of a dream character
- a stone painted stark white to match the dreamer's state of being.

Yes, there are many creative possibilities for exploring your dreams. Where to begin? Anyplace. According to your personal inclinations. Begin with a creative form that is comfortable. When you feel like broadening your comfort zone, surprise yourself. Try something totally new.

This section describes ways to enter your dreams creatively. To begin, imagine you are standing before a set of tall glass doors. Behind these doors you can see your imagery waiting. The moment of epiphany, that moment when you truly know with all of your senses what is true and alive for you, lies in this world behind the glass doors. Over the doors are etched the words "Dreams are the Gateway to Imagination: Adults May Enter Here. Children Already Live Here."

Open the doors. Begin to play creatively with your imagery. Your dream will respond to you. It will emerge from behind its veil of mystery, revealing its layers of meaning. Entering these doors, you are transitioning into dream language. You are communicating with your soul.

Priming the Creative Pump

Free Association

Free association is a simple process that can reveal the hidden meanings of any dream. This is a good exercise to prime the creative pump. Start with the key images in a dream: the characters, objects, situations, and sensory details. Work with one image at a time and jot down whatever comes to mind when you think of this image. Let these associations freely float up to your consciousness without stopping to interpret or judge them. When you have finished, reread the list you have compiled for each image. Notice which association is most compelling, which one evokes an "aha" in you. You may have two associations that share this feeling, which is fine. Once you have free-associated for all the images, step back and make an

4. TRANSFORMING DREAMS INTO CREATIVE EXPRESSIONS

interpretation of this dream. I say "an interpretation" because dreams are layered with meaning. They are not fixed entities; they are fluid and multi-faceted. With each creative exploration a new layer is exposed. This exercise is a quick, easy way to begin your creative exploration, as long as you don't regard it as the only meaning of your dream. For a more detailed description of this process, see the Wheel of Association exercise.

Active Imagination

Every character and symbol in your dreams reveals an aspect of you. Because they come from your interior world, they may surprise you. It is helpful to get to know these characters and symbols, especially the ones you want to disown. You can learn a great deal from them about why they have appeared and what they have to offer to you. Dialoguing with your dream characters is a reliable and simple way to encourage the dream to reveal itself.

Carl Jung used his imagination to access his unconscious and to engage its participation with his conscious mind. The process he used is known as Active Imagination, the art of inner dialogue. An excellent discussion of this process is found in Robert Johnson's *Inner Work*.

Johnson defines four steps: First, you invite the dream figure or symbol to be with you. (Objects are as important as people or animals; I once had an enlightening conversation with a credit card.) Then you dialogue with it. Afterwards, you examine the conversation. Lastly, you establish a ritual or practice.

You will need at least thirty minutes to complete the dialogue.

The first fifteen or twenty minutes of conversation with your dream character enables you to establish a rapport with your unconscious. After that your deeper wisdom will emerge.

The following description of this process evolved from my personal work with Johnson's material.

Step One—Invitation
Find a quiet place, as free of distractions as possible. Bring paper and pen or sit at the computer. Begin with this meditation:

Close your eyes. Come to your breath. Let it rise and fall in a natural way. Be with your breath, letting your mind quiet with each exhalation and inhalation. Take your time. As you breathe, see your mind becoming empty. Imagine your breath carrying you deeper into the world of your imagination. In this quiet place, wait to see who will appear to you. Wait patiently. Nothing may happen immediately.

You may be surprised which dream figure comes to you. It may be the one you were curious about from last night's dream. It may be an entirely new image. Let yourself accept whoever shows up. Let go of your judgments and your quick rejection. Your soul knows more about what you need than your thoughts do.

When your dream figure comes into your awareness, use your five senses (sight, touch, smell, hearing, and taste) to help you perceive the figure or symbol. Ask yourself, what does this figure look like? What is it wearing? What does its skin or surface look like? Can I touch it or smell it? What do I hear? Is there anything here to taste? When you have a strong image and sense impression, you are ready to begin your conversation.

4. TRANSFORMING DREAMS INTO CREATIVE EXPRESSIONS

Step Two—Dialogue

Begin your dialogue with some simple questions. After each question, wait for an answer.

Who are you?

What do you want?

What are you bringing me?

Let go of any desire to control the answers. Wait with an open mind and stay focused on whatever has presented itself. There will be time later to assess the answers.

When the dialogue begins, write down what you ask and what the dream character or symbol says or does. Allow your imagination to write a dialogue between you and the dream character or symbol you have chosen to work with. Allow the dream character to respond to you and visa versa. Perhaps the dream character will want to tell you a story or will continue the dream. Perhaps you and the dream character will argue about a situation.

The important thing is to keep going. Don't stop the dialogue. If you can get past your resistance, illuminating things happen. As Johnson emphasizes, "inviting in" means just that. It doesn't mean "to manage" the process.

What do you do if no dream character appears? You consciously select one, and proceed.

Step Three—Examination

After the dialogue, you can investigate what has been revealed. Some of the imagery may be raw and ugly. Some of it may be tender and poetic. We learned as children to hide what was unacceptable to the adults around us, but our dreams remember. When we engage them, we uncover what we once hid—both the ugly and the tender.

What do we do when unexpected or difficult material appears? First, we evaluate what has been given to us. Rather than repress this material, we want to meet it. Active imagination opens the unconscious depths; we may meet characters with no morality, those parts of ourselves suppressed because of their "badness." Or we may discover exalted characters with bold wisdom. Meet each one with awareness and without judgment.

Our conscious mind listens to this material, choosing whether or not to act on it. If a dream character tells us to do something, we do not have to comply. A dark or evil character is presenting itself to you to be understood, its vitality to be integrated into our lives in a way that fuels our creativity rather than destroys us. Johnson speaks clearly about our responsibility to meet our interior, unconscious selves. "The critical task that each of us has . . . when we 'take the lid off' of the unconscious, is to think independently and clearly. We must listen carefully to hear the truth that is hidden behind the . . . urgings of the inner voices. You must refine the truth to something . . . that can be integrated into ordinary human life without incinerating it. And, toward that truth, you must find your own individual ethical stance." It is helpful to ask your heart to be open and be compassionately present to your pain and distortions so you can learn what needs healing. You then restore the truth and transform the raw, uneven edges.

The conscious and the unconscious need to work together. First

4. TRANSFORMING DREAMS INTO CREATIVE EXPRESSIONS

one leads and the other follows. Then they switch places, continuing this exchange until the hidden and visible worlds become integrated.

Step Four—Ritual

Take what you have received and make it tangible. The key is to honor and remember what your dream character has given you. Creating a ritual will integrate this wisdom into your daily life. Johnson says, "The most powerful rituals are the small ones, the subtle ones. It is not necessary to do big things or expensive things . . . The best rituals are physical, solitary and silent: These are the ones that register most deeply with the unconscious."

■ ■ ■

After I received a dream whose meaning evaded me completely, I did the following Active Imagination process.

Dream: *I have gone away to a retreat place for the weekend. I've just arrived. B. and I are looking for beds. All the cots are out. They have metal frames and no mattresses. Some of the frames have round wires, close together. Others have huge spaces between the wires. You would have to be a very big person to sleep on those. I find a couple of the small wire ones. One of them is in E.'s room. The other is in the more crowded room. I decide to take the one in E.'s room because it will be easy to get into when I come home late.*

Me: Who are you?
Bedsprings: I'm your support.
Me: What kind of support are you?
Bedsprings: You must choose your support. One that has space in

it, but not too much space or you will fall through. You can choose a crowded room with too many people or a small room with one or two others.

Me: Like with E. who is also a poet and a writer.

Bedsprings: Yes, like E. who wants to support you.

Me: But neither choice looks very comfortable.

Bedsprings: That depends on your point of view. From my view it's not about comfort. You humans want to cover up the bed frame with a mattress and hide the structure beneath. You never think about what holds you up. I'm here to make you think about the kind of support you need for your creative life. Without me, you would not take seriously E.'s offer. You would let your obligations interfere with your creativity.

Me: But what about rest? This dream was about picking my place to rest.

Bedsprings: Do you not find rest in your creativity? In your writing and art? Isn't that what we are talking about? Rest from the busy structure of your life?

Me: So what is B. doing in the dream?

Bedsprings: She is a big person with a big aura. She needs a large bed. You are a little person. You have a smaller, quieter aura. You need a smaller bed or else you will fall through the holes. You will lose You. You may think you want to be like her, to do big studies and teach big courses, be so visible, but you are small and will be more comfortable in a smaller space, sharing your creativity quietly with E.

4. TRANSFORMING DREAMS INTO CREATIVE EXPRESSIONS

The conversation with the "bedsprings" came spontaneously. The bedsprings' wisdom made me feel very comfortable with my size and quiet needs. Often I am in a battle between the part of me that wants to be bigger and more visible, and the quieter, gentler part that loves to write and draw and dream. That part was not acceptable or nurtured in my childhood, so I was totally surprised by this dialogue. Processes like these help me wake up and more deeply understand the language of my unique essence.

To complete this process I performed a ritual. I created a collection of small mandalas to nurture my creativity in a quiet way. I also accepted E.'s support.

The dialoguing process is simple and valuable. We all know how to have conversations, and we can dialogue with a dream character anywhere.

Becoming the Symbol

Many dreamers find it helpful to take on the persona of each part of the dream. This means you become the dream characters or symbols, and either speak for them or listen to them. You may find you are continuing the dream. It is best to do this with your eyes closed. You may choose to have a dream helper who will witness and assist you if you get stuck, but will not intrude on your process.

Naomi says this is her favorite way of working with dreams. She describes one she calls "Fire Dream."

"At the time I had this dream, I was teaching a parenting workshop and had an uncomfortable interaction with a co-teacher who, in the past, had always eased my feelings if I thought I had caused a disaster.

I always was looking to an authority to tell me I had done the right or wrong thing. I was afraid I would cause endless devastation if I said one inappropriate thing.

"One night when I was feeling most uncomfortable, I reached for the phone to call her and suddenly remembered a dream from six weeks before.

"I am burning something in a black metal incinerator like they have in England. It seems to be two or three balls of Old Man's Beard (a common English plant). Just as the last flicker is finishing, two neighboring fires start up. After the fires are all put out, I discover both my son and daughter have been burned to death. I am distraught and don't know how I am going to live. Then I start putting things together. It dawns on me that sparks from my fire may have started the two neighboring fires. When they began, it had looked as though they started on their own. BUT I CAN'T BE SURE. I am overcome with guilt that I may have killed my own children. Now I don't know how I am going to live with this. I know it is illegal in America to light fires because it is far too dangerous, and I thought I knew better. All I want is someone to tell me it's not my fault. I decide to discuss it with my husband in the hopes that he can allay my unbearable feeling of guilt.

"One of the people I depended upon to assuage my guilt was the person I was having difficulty with. As I thought about the dream, I realized my imagery around causing destruction is mythical. It's ludicrous that what I might casually say would cause such destruction. The feeling of dread is strong in my body, but not in my mind. When I made this connection, I got the meaning of the dream.

4. TRANSFORMING DREAMS INTO CREATIVE EXPRESSIONS

But I knew I needed to go back into the dream to change this place in me that is out of proportion.

"I took it to my dream group and went back into the dream, where the spirits of my children spoke to me. They said, 'It's okay, Mum, we chose to fight the fire. It was our responsibility to risk death.'

"Then I became the fire. What came out was that I, the fire, was an organic process with no good or bad. I was just burning away. Just by *being* I cause destruction. I realized this equated with my birth. When I was born, my mother was sick and I was sent away from ages eight to eleven months while she got well. I began to understand that my fear of doing something wrong did not come from the reality of making a mistake. It was something I carried with me because along with my birth came chaos in my family, resulting in a recurrence of my mother's illness, called Meniere's Syndrome. This is a disease which amplifies all sounds inside the head to a high degree of discomfort. It is a latent disease, which my crying as an infant caused to flare up.

"I realize that fire is like breathing, just as divine. The baby is no different from the fire. Both are in a state of *being* and are from God. My fear came from my investing the fire with something that didn't actually exist in the fire."

Visual Arts

Dream Painting

Drawing or painting dream imagery can be an exciting way to bring your dreams to life, since most dreams are highly visual. Of course, it is impossible to accurately duplicate dream imagery since it is so intensely vivid, as if from another dimension. Painting your imagery is its own act of creation. When you let the dream inspire your painting, the process and the final piece open up more meanings to the dream.

The dream symbols will be most revealing when the painting design is unplanned. When your hands, eyes, and mind are occupied with colors and shapes, your unconscious is free to reveal itself. Then when you step back from your drawing, you may discover things you did not know about yourself.

In *Art is a Way of Knowing* Pat B. Allen describes a technique she learned from the art therapist Margaret Naumburg. The technique includes writing one's associations, both immediate responses and insights into the future, after completing each painting. Naumburg recommends soaking a large sheet of watercolor paper in the bathtub and then pinning it to an easel board. Using large brushes and acrylic paints, you "let the painting paint itself." When the painting is finished, you write your responses in a loose-leaf notebook, dividing each page in half and using the right side for immediate responses and the left side for future observations.

4. TRANSFORMING DREAMS INTO CREATIVE EXPRESSIONS

How to Begin Your Painting

Sit before a large piece of paper or a canvas, your choice of paints beside you. Quietly review your dream. See which image seems to have the most energy for you at this moment. Take the image that pops into focus. It need not be a main character or symbol. Select a color and then paint a shape that suggests your image. Then see what else you want to include. Let the imagery guide you. Avoid criticizing your work. As in the dialoguing process, keep going even after you want to stop. You may find yourself wanting to paint over part or all of an image. Follow your inner movement. Step back occasionally and see what is emerging. You may find shapes or objects that want to come forward. Let them be discovered. By accentuating this new imagery, you will learn something new about yourself and your dream.

The best media for this type of painting are those that flow easily and do not require training. Chalk pastels, oil pastels, and acrylic and tempera paints are good choices. Markers, crayons, and colored pencils work better for mandalas or small paintings.

A Personal Experience with Dream Painting

Alone on retreat in Bermuda, I decided to paint the inner world of my torn octopus image. I felt vulnerable and open to all my feelings and to my body's sensations. At the same time, I was prepared to face whatever arose from my unconscious. Over several days I painted the wordless anguish I was feeling as I connected my infant self with the torn octopus.

I modified Naumberg's process for my own work. I had brought with me a selection of handmade papers and acrylics. I thought their beautifully deckled edges and smooth surfaces would enrich my wordless paintings. I wanted paper strong enough for layering or scrubbing out images. I also kept a record of the colors and shapes painted on each layer. I created paintings on top of paintings, just like the layers of a dream. The underpaintings were as important to me as the final painting.

Almost simultaneously my feelings burst into words. "I am enraged. Still in the womb. In the channel I've lost my mother! Metal grabs my head. I clench my jaw and die. I am dragged into the world. I hate God. I scream and flail. I swim in a fiery sea. It is all I know. I no longer feel pain."

In my first painting the underpainting evokes the spirit world and the womb: it is iridescent white and shimmery pale yellow, with a golden eye in the center. The overpainting is red and burnt umber. The golden eye gleams through the red sea. I title this painting Red Eye.

Each day I listen to my feelings and my body's sensations. I paint, and then write about the feelings of the painting. The shimmery spirit world eye is still visible in the next painting, slashed with swaths of fiery red. "All my cries are in my heart. I am quieted by the energy of the doctor at my birth."

The third underpainting is opalescent white and yellow and over it, the pale blue of a tender sky. "I weep at the memory of floating gently. I reach for the hollow in my heart, the cavern of destiny." Gray, umber, dark blue, burnt sienna, and red cover the tender sky. I shape broken bits of blue and green plastic, found on the beach, into an eye. "Swirling anguish descends. Night closing in on my soul, but my eye is clear and refuses to surrender. The edges are fuzzy. My eye is broken. I am battered." I title this Eye Shall Behold My New World.

To begin the fourth painting, I smear all the remaining colors on my palette from the last painting onto a new canvas. I set the painting aside. I walk the beach. I feel raw and tender from this practice. What keeps me going is my knowledge that I will move through this darkness into a place of light and clarity.

I return. Over the dark smears, I paint blue-green waters, then a whirling black hole. I experience great pleasure swirling the paint-laden brush around. "I am only weeks old. The jail doors are slamming shut. There is nowhere to go. No rescue. No one to see that I am broken and falling into an abysmal place."

It's a great pleasure to paint everything with black and to frame it with slabs of red. I name it The Passionate Abyss.

The next one begins with a white whirlpool. "From the infant's view, a purplish blackness with the knuckles and fingers of a hand, claw-like, crawls up out of the dark. The hand is putrid. A thick gray window waits behind the hand. As far as the eye can see, the heart is flattened."

I set it aside and begin a new canvas, gray first, then a sheer white. "I must know the light places which are still within me, hidden. I need hope. In the flat gray, where is hope?" Over the sheer white I paint iridescent white angel wings. "Who can bear the pain of covering up these exquisite wings? I cannot bear things going away, ending, leaving, OVER, dead."

I cover the wings with more gray. "I go out in the world, living with gray. The sky outside gray, too. I know gray and I am alive." For the first time I feel comfortable with the grayness in my life. I don't try to cover it up with gaiety or activity. Covered Angel Wings is this painting's title.

I am ready for Bermuda colors. "Where I'm going, it is sometimes blue-green waters and sometimes pink sands, but its purity is mixed with gray and wind. Life is neither all desolation nor all perfect waters. I live in both, riding the waves up and down, sailing on the wind, blowing with the sand."

On the last day I dream *of my friend who has been caring for a baby for a long time. She goes to court to adopt the baby, who calls her mother. But the court says she is too radical to be the child's mother. My friend says, "I'm not a radical. I'm a revolutionary." She looks like my Tai Chi teacher. She is Jewish, and she and the baby eat leftover pizza from the Spanish maid. They play hula hoop in the street late at night. I wonder what my parents would say about my being friends with a revolutionary.*

After I return home, I paint a gray octopus being healed by a shadowy woman, and an immense skeleton behind it. Later I see the skeleton's resemblance to the octopus. It stands in strong contrast to my first bright, playful watercolors of octopuses. Those whimsical images were my fantasy of the octopus. Now I have painted the white skull/octopus to bring it before the Divine Presence for healing. I am following my radical, revolutionary way to true wholeness, not content to live the mask of the whimsical octopus world.

Two months later I realize I have completed my exploration of the torn octopus world. I trusted myself to enter the dark night of my birth, to know my earliest broken connection and my hidden anguish. I discovered a world of expression that I thought was lost. I took pleasure in the tactile and visual sensations of painting. In the end, I experienced my own resurrection. I knew myself as my own radical savior.

The Mandala

> The Vegetative Universe, opens like a flower from the Earths center:
> In which is Eternity.
>
> —William Blake
> *Jerusalem*: Plate 13:34-35

The mandala is one of my favorite creative expressions. Even at its simplest, its aura is that of mystery and power. A mandala is an ancient, archetypal symbol of wholeness and unity found in many cultures. It holds the whole universe, good and bad. Its traditional design was a circle enclosing a square or a square enclosing a circle. This sacred circle was symmetrically balanced in four sections; sometimes it included concentric circles.

The word *mandala* is Sanskrit for circle, or magic circle. It also means essence, center, and circumference. The mandala is sacred space. Into that space you invite your highest self, the center of your being. The mandala touches all of you with its essence, just as the center reaches out and touches the rest of the mandala.

In the East elaborate mandalas filled with geometrical shapes have been created for centuries as sacred art. An ancient mandala ritual is still practiced by Buddhist monks, who spend days together creating mandalas of sand. After the mandala is completed, they ritually disperse every grain of sand. In this meditative act of creation and destruction, Buddhists declare the impermanence of life and illustrate the importance of the process, rather than the product. In the United States Southwest, the Navajo people create sand mandalas for healing.

In its simplest and most common form, the mandala consists of a circle in which you draw a design. The circle is found in all of nature. It is the sun, moon, earth, the center of a flower, the body of an octopus, the eye, and the rhythm of the seasons. The circular pattern is a universal form which appears in all cultures.

Carl Jung introduced the use of the mandala to Western psychology. Through his research he discovered the presence of the mandala throughout history and in many cultures. He chose to use the Sanskrit name for this archetypal form.

In his autobiography *Memories, Dreams, Reflections* Jung describes his personal exploration of the mandala's revelatory, healing properties. It began at the end of World War I. His break with Freud a few years earlier, along with the war, had plunged him into turmoil and disorientation. Every morning he sketched a small mandala, which he said, "seemed to correspond to my inner situation at the time. With the help of these drawings I could observe my psychic transformations from day to day." It was also during this time that he came to understand that the "goal of psychic development is the self. There is no linear evolution; there is only a circumambulation of the self." He realized that "everything was directed toward the center."

Towards the end of World War I, he gradually emerged from his darkness. He attributed this emergence, in part, to beginning to

4. TRANSFORMING DREAMS INTO CREATIVE EXPRESSIONS

understand the healing significance of mandala drawings. He "guarded [them] like precious pearls," and from them says he experienced inner peace. After he stopped making mandalas, he turned his attention to the traditions of the cultures that used the mandala, to better understand its effects on the human psyche. He discovered that the mandala—drawn, painted, or carved in stone—is present in most wisdom traditions. Understanding the mandala as the representation of the whole self, he offered it to his clients as an aid in their individuation, the process of becoming distinct and whole individuals. He described the mandala as "the archetype of inner order . . . [which] expresses the fact that there is a center and a periphery, and it tries to embrace the whole." He believed that the act of making the mandala was more important than the completed product.

Another famous creator of mandalas was Hildegard of Bingen, a twelfth century abbess who had many mystical visions, which she was afraid to share with others. Then she became ill and realized that her fear was the source of the illness. Overcoming that fear, she recorded her visions, painted mandalas, and healed herself. She began to live all her talents, becoming a theologian, musician, poet, physician, dramatist, and scientist. As a teacher, she emphasized the central role of creativity in human spiritual life.

Today, Judith Cornell, an artist and teacher, has refined the process of mandala work for healing. She uses meditation, the mantra Aum, light, and energy in her healing work, and recommends creating illuminated mandalas using black paper and white and colored pencils. She suggests you begin the process by blessing your art materials and visualizing light and energy flowing through your hands and pencils. Her book, *Mandala*, shows her methods for making this sacred art. She describes the process as "creating a temple [where] we make the invisible visible."

When we create a mandala, we are reaching into the wordless place within us to remind us that the healing of the self is a circular process. Our healing continually leads us inward to the universal center.

How to Create a Mandala From Your Dream Imagery

You will need these basic supplies and 30-60 minutes of quiet time:

- paper
- colored markers, crayons or paints
- a circular pattern that fits the size of your paper, such as a paper plate

Sit quietly in a place where you will not be disturbed; the longer the time you have, the more relaxed you will be. You may want to begin by lighting a candle and offering a prayer. Or you might simply reread your dream. Sit quietly, and then invite your highest self into the process. Be with the dream for a few minutes. When you are ready, ask for a statement of intention toward the dream, or a question that the dream triggers. Write this on the back of the paper. Return to your quiet space. Throughout the process, stay as aware of yourself as possible without analyzing what is happening. Sense with your body the strongest point of the dream imagery. Wait until you have a clear image, color, or shape.

4. TRANSFORMING DREAMS INTO CREATIVE EXPRESSIONS

Whenever you feel ready, select a color and use it to draw a circle on your paper around the paper plate. The circle is merely a guiding shape for the mandala. There are no absolute directives here, such as keeping your artwork within the circle. The shape your mandala takes will arise from your dream and you.

You can start your drawing in the center or at any point in the circle, but let the mandala lead you. The shapes or symbols will come. If you get stuck, stop and wait. The next step will present itself. Keep drawing or painting until you know your mandala is finished. Set it in front of you. Sit quietly or take a moment to stretch. You might want to turn the mandala and look at it from different perspectives.

Return to your dream. Write down any associations you have to your mandala. Sense what it is saying to you. Listen to your body. If another question or statement arises, write it down. You can use this to create a second mandala. Before you begin another mandala, take a few moments to savor the process you have just finished. Be sure to date and title your mandala.

Mandala Variations

1. The Inspiraling Mandala

I once watched a woman in one of my dream workshops write a long message to herself, winding it through her painting. Her creation inspired me to combine writing with the mandala form. For me, it was a perfect marriage of art and writing, and a way to go beyond my controlling mind and deeper into Spirit.

Begin this process with an intention, written on the back of your paper. Next wait for an image to appear. Draw it in the center of a large sheet of paper. Then begin to write, starting at the outer edge. Write in a circle, turning the paper as you go, until you have spiraled deeply into your psyche.

For several months before my first inspiraling mandala, I had been working with a dream. In the dream *I was stuck in the snow, where I had a choice between going to Cheyenne or Shoshone.* I had explored the cultures of both tribes and their contrasting ways of life. This made it possible to choose clearly. The Cheyenne were hunters and warriors. The Shoshone were peaceful people who traveled in small groups, gathering plants to eat. In the winter, many Shoshone clans gathered together to sing, dance, and tell stories.

At the time I had this dream, I was accustomed to living with my energy revved up. When I explored this dream, a Shoshone woman came out of the shadows to offer me a way of being. Making a mandala elicited her wisdom. In the circle I drew a nest of blue eggs, and placed brown slanted walls on each side of the paper. Then, moving from the outer edges into the center, I began to spiral the Shoshone woman's words:

"A delicate balance I give to you. In the heart of shining light when the walls fall in upon one another and you tumble towards chaos, I am there offering you a nest of small twigs to hold the fragile blue egg growing at the seat of your soul. I will cushion your fragile, new life, teaching you the wonders and passions of simplicity until you are ready to be born and to fly into the dazzling sunlight. I am Shoshone woman, content with the simple life, living out the circular round of my existence, traveling the land from one food source to another, surrounded by the most sensual landscape, riches and indulgences of sight and sound and texture. I do not understand the white woman's disconnection from the source of all being. Your center abides in the simplicity of the egg. Let the veils drop. Fall through the collapsing walls. Disintegrate and be reborn. This day you are anew, traveling in the land from painting to painting, from word to word. All that matters is sun, moon, robin's egg, my heart and yours. Walk gently. Take only what you need. Speak little. Listen for the wind. Receive the sun's penetrating heat and the silver light of the moon to guide you in the black night, for the Creator never abandons us, only dims the light that we may sharpen our vision."

2. The Autobiographical Mandala

One way to honor your dreams is to paint their images within a circular shape. The shape of the mandala cradles the whole self and evokes the ever-moving wheel of life.

Janice painted a large mandala filled with her current imagery: a door open to the world; a dancing bear in the doorway; a tree growing outside, its limbs branching inside the house and turning into antlers; a nest in the center of the tree; a turtle coming out of the swirling wind; a hawk; the sun rising; a rumpled bed with a snake crawling out from under it; curtains blowing at the window, and a bat clinging to them. Over the bed was a stoplight, the green light on. The final image she painted was that of herself holding her passport, emerging from her chrysalis.

"This painting summarizes what working with my dreams did for me. The doors opened and a lot of things came into my life—many images, many dreams. The dream is saying, 'Your time of sleeping is over. It's time to go ahead. The door is open.' I woke up and found I had emerged from the chrysalis. I had never painted a mandala before. This painting showed me the magic of the dream world. These are all my friends."

Collage

1. Basic Collage

A collage is a painting created by cutting and pasting images and words together. It is especially good to use with a long dream. You will need a variety of magazines and printed materials with visual images. Begin with your dream imagery. As you search your collection, let yourself choose images and words that evoke the feeling of the dream. Trust your selection. Also, you can draw or paint images to combine with what you have selected. To assemble your collage, lay everything in front of you.

You can overlap images or leave spaces between them. Also, you can fill the spaces with colored papers, paint or markers. There are no rules in collage; one simply experiments with images, texture, color and shape. As you design your collage, you are making connections between seemingly disparate images. The result often offers a startling new way of seeing yourself.

In a way, we are mimicking dreams when we make a collage. Dreams are a mixture of elements that our logical minds would never

4. TRANSFORMING DREAMS INTO CREATIVE EXPRESSIONS

put together. Symbols that may not seem connected, when placed together, give us new insights in a quick, compelling way.

2. Tissue Paper Collage

Colored tissue paper works beautifully as a collage medium. You can create these collages right in your dream journal. All you need is a package of art tissue and a bottle of paper glue. Begin with the major dream symbols. Select colors to represent these symbols and tear the tissue into shapes. You can design the piece before gluing the shapes into the journal, or you can work spontaneously, gluing down the shapes as you go. You can overlap the pieces to create depth and shadow. Work quickly, allowing your unconscious to reveal itself.

Ann Sayre Wiseman, a professor at Lesley College, uses collage to create dream maps. The following is based on her work. Starting with your dream, you create a map of its inner landscape using torn pieces of colored tissues. When you have finished your collage, you dialogue with yourself:

What do you like or dislike about the situation you have depicted?

How does it resemble your life?

What do you need to do to change things?

After you answer these questions, you dialogue with the symbols in the dream. Then you tear new shapes and add them to the collage. As you alter it, you are allowing a new possibility to arise and make its place in your life.

Sculpture

Sometimes a dream calls for a three-dimensional creation. There are many media that make modeling easy for the nonprofessional artist, such as white or gray self-hardening or non-hardening clay, or brightly colored Sculpee. Give yourself plenty of time to make your sculpture. Do it slowly, making contact with your deep self. Try using modeling beeswax, which comes in many vivid colors. This rich substance must be warmed in your hands to soften. You can either sit in meditation with your dream, holding the beeswax in your hands; or listen to music while you knead it. When the wax becomes pliable, it can be thinned to create very delicate shapes.

Mixed Media

A dream has many dimensions. Its parts do not relate to each other rationally or logically. They are discontinuous. Nonlinear, often fantastical, and full of feeling, a dream lends itself to expression through a combination of mediums. Liz, whose work was described in the chapter on spiritual dream practice, uses dreams as inspiration for her artwork. Recently she has been creating works of mixed media, combining her dream-inspired poems with sculpture, audiotapes, and slides. The effect is kaleidoscopic. Her works are so vivid and mobile that her dreams seem to have come suddenly alive and to have entered the room.

4. TRANSFORMING DREAMS INTO CREATIVE EXPRESSIONS

Creative Writing

I didn't trust it for a moment,
but I drank it anyway,
the wine of my own poetry.

It gave me the daring to take hold
of the darkness and tear it down
and cut it into little pieces.

—Lalla
Translated by Coleman Barks

Dreams are a rich source of material for all kinds of writing—journal entries, epigrams, essays, short stories, novels, plays, or poetry. The dream is the entry point; writing then reveals depths of the ego's incapabilities.

I wrote the following piece at the end of a long imaginal dialogue I did with Princess Diana, who had appeared in a dream. It came from a part of myself that I often forget in the complexity of daily living. Judith Gendler's *Book of Qualities* was my inspiration for this type of writing. What I wrote opened my narrow beliefs about sorrow. Its simplicity softened my resistance to knowing sorrow.

"Sorrow is a strong woman, robust, short, with strong legs. She stands close to the earth, and she can travel through heavy snows across the mountains. She knows where the pass is, even when it is buried under ice and snow. She is an angel of mercy. She is patient, knowing that you will one day pass this way. She does not regret her task, or try to leave it. She accepts her responsibilities with a quiet fortitude and gentle sense of humor. She loves grief, just as she loves the blue sky on piercingly cold days. She appreciates the many hues of grief, like the variegated colors of white that snow reflects in the changing light of each day."

Writing from a dream bypasses the critical mind and opens the heart. A paragraph or two can be a powerful way to honor a dream. This will anchor the dream's message in your consciousness.

Free Writing

Writing freely from a dream, you may find that you have the beginning of a story or a novel. This dream inspired a long piece of free writing, which I could now develop into a story.

I am witness to the death of Orson Welles, one of the last great actors. My friends and I are watching him perform. He is crippled with age, yet suddenly we see him gamboling over the hillside. We say to each other, "This can't be him. He must have just taken a drug." Suddenly he falls. My friends rush to his side. He is saying the dying words of a major Shakespearean character. He has dropped his glasses and cannot see. I saw them fall and I go to get them just as he begins the death scene, saying, "I am dying. I am dying." Then he is gone. We have witnessed, with awe, the last breath, beyond words. This is history.

Here are excerpts from my free writing of this dream:

"He died the death of a conscious dreamer, suddenly, seemingly unprepared by a long illness for death, gamboling across the hillside, so unlike his lately crippled state.

"'The day is right for dying,' he said to his companion as they climbed the hill. Arduously, he took each step, determined to reach the crest of even this lump of earth. He could climb mountains in his youth, carrying pounds of equipment on his back, stronger even than his sons in their prime of blooming youth. Now the smallest step brought screams of pain to his brain. I am old at last, he thought. My body is like an old, rusty chainsaw, refusing to cut another tree, yet being forced by an unseen power to cut down one last mighty oak.

"I have entered into dying fully aware that I, me, my essence, my whole being is beyond physicality. I have begun to leave my body. My crippled body straightens. My step lightens. I am prancing like a lamb leaping in the spring sun, delighted to be born. My friends cannot keep up with me. I am leaping into Spirit.

"I see the earth and sky peaked to a brilliance I have not remembered since childhood. I am seeing it from the perspective of spirit, unbounded by a body. I leap. I dance. I step lightly to the tune only I hear, the song of rejoicing.

"All too soon my legs stumble, my glasses fall, I thud to the earth, thrust back into my crippled body. I am dying. Those moments of grace were in the next world. I have returned to this world to die. All humans must die. It is our birthright to die. There is no escaping, no leaping off into the great hereafter.

"My friend cradles my head. I begin Hamlet's dying speech, the one I have treasured and spoken many times on the stage. It comes to my lips, unbidden, as knowingly as if I had written it myself, the only way I can tell the world around me what is happening, for they are not wanting to think that Orson Welles would die.

"My words are firm and full of resolution. No one can stop this descent. A force greater than my own will has hold now, and I can only give those who must follow me one day my last great performance, to carry them through the seemingly treacherous gate of death. Now it no longer seems so treacherous. I have cavorted in the sunlight. I am cavorting toward God, leaping across the void that separates this world from the flood of light, from the place without words that poets and musicians seek to evoke. None of my friends can grasp its particular quality. Only I know it exists. All my knowing I pour into this, my last performance."

Poetry

Writing poetry was a mysterious process for me until I realized my dream images were metaphors which could be expressed in poetry. This was a wonderful "aha" for me. In college I had majored in English and loved poetry. I had even taught English for several years. But I had never explored writing poetry. If you, too, think you cannot write poetry, set that belief aside for a moment. Play with the images from your most insistent dreams. Avoid censoring or editing. Let the images write through you. Feel their power. Write freely without stopping to edit yourself before you refine your poem.

I had several desert dreams one winter while I was ill with bronchitis. I was intent on finding the emotional source of my chronic illness, but I resisted acknowledging that it was deep grief. The desert I dreamed was my state of depression, which I could not name at the time.

4. TRANSFORMING DREAMS INTO CREATIVE EXPRESSIONS

In the first dream *a desert prophet appeared. I am wearing my hair in an Afro with letters carved in it. These letters spell a shortened form of Muhammad. I am the only white person in my class to do this. I am a bit embarrassed, but I have been wearing my hair this way for months.*

Sometimes when you start to work with a dream, similar dreams will appear. The second dream came a week later. I titled it "Going into the Desert." *I am staying in a hotel with a caretaker, and we have a free day. I go to the hotel clerk for ideas; he suggests we drive into the desert where Moses spent his life. Part of it is desert and part is swollen with rains. The caretaker tells me to come back in January and go into the desert for the whole month. It seems I want to do a paper on Moses. I feel daunted at the thought of going there alone, but my companion, the caretaker, is ill. He says, "I have never had such a long time of contact and intimacy with another person." All he wants to do is weep. I say, "The desert must wait."*

The third desert dream followed a week later. I titled it "Watching from the Pueblo." *A woman enters an underground cave and goes into a volcano-like rage. I am watching this from above ground in a pueblo in the desert. Her rage rocks the ground as she does expressive work around her mother and father. A very handsome, stocky, sexy man comes to sit by me and I feel safe. We know each other. He knows there's a mystery here. We are trying to unravel it. Some travelers from outer space may have coded the kids in this pueblo, and they still carry the codes. I am attracted to him like a magnet.*

Because I have a Judeo-Christian background, Moses was part of my childhood, but not Muhammad. All I knew was that he was a major prophet. I had been told in my childhood that the line of Islam came from the split between the brothers Esau and Jacob, which occurred after Jacob stole Esau's inheritance. For some time, my dreams had alluded to the theft of my creative inheritance.

In the first dream I am daring to reclaim my inheritance by wearing my hair in an Afro with Muhammad carved in it. Free-associating, I came up with the following words: daring, wild, breaking out, unconventional, mystery, fire.

Then I reentered the other two dreams imaginally and drew those journeys. In the first, I went into the desert; in the second, I walked on a boardwalk until it ended, and I was afraid to go farther. I knew the desert of my life was waiting for me and that I, like Moses, must cross this desert to the Promised Land. I was afraid that I, like Moses, would never reach my destination. I drew the desert, the boardwalk, and the underground volcano that I had dammed up so that it could only leak, but never flow steadily. I looked at how I was avoiding the desert and underground cave. The handsome man represented all the ways I had done that. I felt as though I had been coded since childhood, and was now searching for a way to decipher those codes. One way was to write poetry.

Here is one of a series of poems I wrote:

Desert Sands

The desert awaits
its sands hot and dry.
Like Muhammad I go to meet myself
his name carved in the bushes of my hair.
I can travel as far as the boardwalk goes.
Beyond that lies sleep.

4. TRANSFORMING DREAMS INTO CREATIVE EXPRESSIONS

I trudge one small hill of sand.
It is all I can do alone.
Then I descend rapidly into not knowing,
drunk with resistance.
Who could wander these hills for forty years
and not give up hope?
I am not Moses.
I cannot wander for forty seconds.
Without a destination, I am hopeless.
In the desert all I do is dream of being elsewhere.
I would rather descend into an underground cave,
spouting with water from a mysterious source than
bear the weight of my deserted heart.

Then I had another dream. In it I was told, *"If you drink cream, you will store up enough fat and energy to cross the desert."* Instantly I knew what I must do to prepare for this journey. My cream is silence, art, and writing. Giving myself "my cream" will make the journey possible. Without it, my life is a desert where I will die.

Two years later I dreamed that *the code was finally broken.* I wasn't afraid of going into the desert: I was terrified of being "deserted." The work I had done with the dreams, including the poems I had written, had been gestating for two years. Now the answer was delivered.

Epitaphs of Dream Characters

Once I dreamed *of a small, old man who was dying. His circulation was leaving his body, from the feet up—only his lungs were left. He lay on a table as several men tried to save him. Then the dream switched: I am his wife. He is lying on top of me, dying, his head on my right shoulder, next to my head. I haven't a lot of feelings for him; I simply hold him as he slowly dies.*

After the dream I wanted to write an elegy for the old man, so I imagined what his life had been like.

> "He was a child of the earth who wanted only to stay put, living on one plot, seeing the seasons turn from winter to spring. But he was born to nomads, who packed up their pickup truck the minute he made friends or planted flowers. They moved on, dragging their possessions behind them, tattered, flapping in the wind. He lost himself in their journey and never knew what it meant to return home. Years later, when he had married and settled down in one place to raise children, his wife asked him where he had gone. He had no answers, no knowledge about where his soul resided, on what mountain vista or canyon bed. He did not even know where to begin the search. His folks had left no markers. Even in death they had been scattered on the wind. And so his wife kept her silence, fed the kids, and went on. When he died, resting upon her chest, she buried him behind the house, on a small rise, beside a lilac bush he loved. She marked his grave, 'Here lies a good man. Come home at last.'"

Writing this elegy, I recognized my basic nature is to live quietly, simply, close to the earth. I have lived like a nomad without roots, "scattered on the wind." I am trying to gather my scattered self through my dreams, art, and therapy. I am listening to my soul's yearning. I do not want to die without having fulfilled this essential call.

4. TRANSFORMING DREAMS INTO CREATIVE EXPRESSIONS

Meditation

Meditation is the practice of stillness and awareness. Dream meditation is a more active process than traditional Eastern and Western sitting practices. In dream meditation you focus quietly on a dream and its symbols, while loosening the mind to allow other images and realizations to arise. It is a paradoxical state: You are both focused and spacious. It is helpful, but not necessary, to have some experience with other types of meditation that quiet your mind and energy. As you work with the process of dream meditation, you will develop your own style.

Find a place where you can be alone for twenty or thirty minutes. You may want to light a candle or burn incense. Before you begin the meditation, read what you wrote about your dream. Sit quietly, clearing your mind of any distractions. Focus on your dream. When your mind gets distracted or wanders, return to the dream.

Move slowly through the imagery and the dream story, staying with each part as long as you need in order to relax your unconscious. Accept everything that comes, without judgment. You need not react to what appears. Whenever you sense yourself rejecting something, focus on your breath, let go, and open to the next thing. Allow your dream to speak to you. It may do this through words, or feelings, or sensations, or new images, or song. When you come out of your meditation, write or draw what came to you during that time.

This kind of active meditation can be practiced in the presence of another person who acts as your secretary, recording your images and thoughts as they arise. This allows you to go deeper because you do not have to switch back and forth from meditation to writing.

A commitment to seven days of meditation on the same dream will deepen your experience of the dream. It will allow your waking self to become a true partner of the soul self, which sent you the dream.

Movement

All our dreams come out of a wordless place; they appear in our consciousness by picture, sound, and movement. It is we who give words to them. To engage with their essence, we can express them non-verbally through movement. We don't have to do this by mimicking the actions of a dream character. We can do this by moving in a way that expresses the kinesthetic sense of the dream. Our expressions can be harsh, wild, delicate or bold.

To reenter the dream through movement, first spend a few minutes quietly, traveling through the dream, remembering how it felt. Holding that sensory memory, begin to move. Allow your movements to emerge from inside your body, not from your head. Your mind will hold the dream. Continue a movement until the next movement naturally succeeds it or a new dream image arises. Move through each feeling in the dream.

Do not stop when you first think you are finished. This may be your resistance, which often arises when you are about to break through to a deeper place of knowing. Just notice the desire to stop, and continue the movement. When you are truly complete, stop and be still. You may want to draw or write about your experience. You may want to select music and shift into a second phase of dream movement.

4. TRANSFORMING DREAMS INTO CREATIVE EXPRESSIONS

The nonverbal expression of a dream resonates in the deepest place within you. Through movement, your dream has the opportunity to ground itself in your cells, to bypass your ego's resistance and to deliver its ineffable message.

Movement becomes even more powerful in the presence of a witness. The witness honors the power of the nonverbal truth. The witness becomes the temple walls, observing the unfolding of a holy communion. Later the witness can reflect back to you what it was like to be present nonverbally to your deep dream.

As you open your breathing and your throat, sound may accompany your movements. The dream may want to speak from your throat or your belly. You may want to accompany it with music. Improvise and follow your own expressive way. Movement does not require a large physical space. Your movements will adapt to whatever space is available.

Movement need not be solo work; two or more dreamers can move or dance to their individual dream feelings in the same space and notice how their collective movements inform each other.

A Conscious Dreamer: Janice

Janice is a creative woman who naturally brings passion to her dreamwork. She had never done any artwork until she came to one of my dream classes.

Janice describes that encounter, "When you brought markers and crayons into that first dream class, the whole world opened up to me. Then you told us that transformation takes place in the act of creating your images and visions. I experimented with that, and behold more images appeared, an overwhelming amount at first. The door opened and a flood happened. In my waking moments I began to see things symbolically. I experienced my symbols in a concrete, rather than abstract way.

"I drew some images, I danced some. I ignored a lot of them. I talked and thought about many of them. The images came faster than the time I had to honor them."

Janice is a physical therapist who has been living with chronic fatigue syndrome the last ten years. In order to get the sleep she needs, she altered the way she lives. She now devotes much more time to her inner life.

"This dream process helped me deal with . . . a frustrating illness. I have lived so close with it. Now living closely with the symbols of my life, I don't feel so dominated by my illness. It has shifted my narrow focus on the physical into another place. This dream work has augmented the spiritual energy I already had. It's been a beautiful experience. The worst of my chronic fatigue now seems to be over."

Janice's creative work with two important dreams led her deeply

4. TRANSFORMING DREAMS INTO CREATIVE EXPRESSIONS

into one of her core issues, and to the practice of prayerful rituals. Though she had these dreams two years apart, she discovered their intimate connection through her focused creative work.

"The first painting I ever did was from a night dream of a nautilus shell. I painted a large mandala of a hand holding a blue nautilus. Then I added my own personal symbols to the painting, one in each of the four directions: a golden hawk's head on the left, the crescent moon to the right, the red bear's claw on the top, and my hand holding the nautilus on the bottom.

The dream: *I was sitting with my son and husband on the edge of a rather wide part of a slow-moving stream. I dove in and on the bottom I found a nautilus. I came out of the water carrying it aloft in my hand. I was awed at how beautiful it was. I recognized it. It had been mine, and nobody thought it was that significant or wonderful or important. It had gotten lost. I came out of the water carrying it, and I offered it to my husband. He hardly noticed and didn't want it. I gave it to my son, and he didn't want it either. I went back to the shore and began to question if it really was that beautiful and whether I wanted to keep it. Nobody important to me recognized how beautiful it was. Now I was questioning it, too. It took my breath away when I first saw it. It was extremely beautiful. The dream ended with me holding it, feeling sad, and not knowing whether I wanted to keep it.*

"When I first had this dream, I thought it was insignificant. However, I honored it by writing it down. That helped me recognize its importance, so then I painted the most careful watercolor I've ever tried to do. I even used protractors to measure every part of the spiral. After I painted it, I realized the image would have come out just as well freehand, but the image was imprinting itself on me through my efforts to get it just right. It engraved itself in me.

"In the dream the stream was very dark and muddy. The nautilus came out of this very organic bottom, yet it had this light to it. I let the nautilus be a symbol of myself. I have to value the beauty I see. I can't throw my work out because someone else doesn't appreciate it.

"I painted the hawk in the East because he came to me in my first shamanic journey. I painted the black crescent moon later. Now I see it is the color of the dark spiral, reflecting light and dark. The bear claw is courage, which I need to go on this journey. When the painting was finished, I mounted it. On the back I am recording thoughts and journeys related to the spiral. I have been wearing blue clothing, as well.

"Many things are birthed in this spiral. It can be pitch black and circle down into the earth, into a place of not knowing. In one of my dream groups, I painted myself half black and half white, and wrote a poem about my ambivalence about *going in* here, and having no choice, either it's now or later. *Going in* means all of the emotional situations I would like to avoid because they are fearful. But that's only part of it. *In* is whatever is. It's the whole thing, everything I live in order to be present in my life. It's being able to stay with whatever is going on.

"I also wrote a long poem called *Conversation with a Nautilus*. It includes these stanzas:

> It's hard, you know, too hard.
> I could die in this birthing.
> "Perhaps. Into your waiting, Lady,
> Push deep."

4. TRANSFORMING DREAMS INTO CREATIVE EXPRESSIONS

Round and round I unravel
edging silence—to be only—ordinary.
How insulting.
"Ah, yes."

"Breathe in. Breathe out.
till the waters of mercy are broken
toward a light that has no quarrel
with your dark."

"After I wrote this poem, the idea of a walking labyrinth came to me, so I made my own in the woods. I go there every day. I sing myself into the center, flying with the hawk so my power animal is with me in prayer.

"Then I made a collage with a black circle spiraling down into the earth. The spiral has become more of a winding cave down into the earth. The black cave comes to mind when I'm feeling strong emotions, when I'm confused, upset, or scared. When I feel lost, I visualize this spiral cave.

"Both the outer and inner worlds are in the nautilus poem. This was the first time my inner world had a form or landscape for me. Before, I thought of it only in terms of thoughts I had. In some ways the journey starts over every moment, every day. Having a form gives me a direction to travel in a world that is not as much a part of our senses."

Janice's work with a second dream deepened her work with the spiral. She called this dream "Bones and Tears."

"I woke from a dream and knew I had been sobbing in it. In the dream *I was going through a pile of bones. My mother, my first husband, and my son as an infant were around the pile. They all had cancer of the bone, and I was frantic to find the cancer in this big pile of bones. I was crying as I searched.*

"I knew these were the three major people I had 'hurt to the bone' by not loving them well. I felt guilty and afraid I had damaged them permanently. A day later, the heaviness of this dream was still with me. I was sitting in meditation and I couldn't stand the weight of it. I leaped out of the chair to fling it off and that's when the dance came. I put on 'The Temptation of Christ,' which has no lyrics. It's passionate Middle Eastern music. I made an imaginary pile of bones in front of me. I invited my mother, son, and first husband to be there in spirit. I began to dance and cry. Pretty soon I thought of others I had seemingly hurt and invited their spirits and lit the bones on fire. It was a big crowd. I cried and danced around a pile of bones. Then I realized there was a second circle of people who had seemingly hurt me. Then another circle of people who had hurt them, until everyone who had ever lived was dancing with me. The big pile of bones became a cremation pyre.

"Even before this Dance of Forgiveness, related images had come to me. I made a crayon mandala, called 'The Wheel of Bones' with tears between the bones, blue flowers around the outside and the words 'Forget Me Not' and 'Je Me Souviens.' I made a collage of bleached chicken bones, tissue paper and gold foil, which increased the power further. I used images of grief, jubilance, Native American Kokopelli, and a figure Diego Rivera did of a creature on all fours, which looked like the most agonizing image I could make.

4. TRANSFORMING DREAMS INTO CREATIVE EXPRESSIONS

"Forgiveness has become an ongoing practice. The dream, my dance, and the collage made it possible for me to own and allow and receive forgiveness. This is a lifetime practice. I knew this when I did the collage. I drew myself as the dancing Zen skeleton on the back. I'm slapping my knee and laughing from the belly. 'Death always wins, yet we need not be defeated.'

"The blue nautilus, the bones of forgiveness, and gratitude have all come together for me. The nautilus has been a metaphor for my illness. I've finally been able to express my gratitude for what it has given me.

"I wear turquoise leather slippers lined with white fringe whenever I am doing 'connecting' work—in dream circles and in my personal sessions. The image of the slippers came to me one morning soon after the bones dream. Before I went to bed, I was looking at the sad face of my son in his childhood pictures. I felt so bad that I wasn't able to give my son a better start in life. I was comfortless. The next morning I woke up having heard a voice saying, 'Put on turquoise slippers.' It was as if my dream were comforting me.

"Oh, this has to do with another dream I had the other night . . ."

And so Janice moves passionately toward the next dream image, knowing there will be a connection between it, her creation, and the dreams that preceded it.

5

Incubating a Dream

In Impossible Darkness

Do you know how
the caterpillar
turns?

Do you remember
what happens
inside a cocoon?

You liquefy.

There in the thick black
of your self-spun womb,
void as the moon before waxing,

you melt

... (as Christ did
for three days
in the tomb) ...

congealing
in impossible darkness
the sheer
inevitability
of wings.

—Kim Rosen

What is Incubation?

The full meaning of a dream does not yield to analysis, or come forth from any of the creative efforts described in the last chapter. At some point the dream or image must incubate. We must let go of our efforts and trust in the power of the image to transform us. This is when the deeper significance of the dream develops quietly.

Incubation is a time of hidden growth, when what is soon to be born is preparing itself for emergence into the light of consciousness. Seeds go through this process before they sprout. Caterpillars incubate in cocoons before they emerge as butterflies. Eggs must be incubated in order for chicks and goslings to be born. The womb is a living incubator enabling all of us to develop from a fertilized egg. When humans are born too early, in an underdeveloped stage, they are placed in incubators that maintain the conditions for further growth and development.

The word *incubation* comes from the Latin root word *incubare*, meaning "to lie down upon." Ancient Greeks respected the wisdom and healing power of dreams. They would come to one of the many temples of Aesculapius to seek healing. Jungian analyst Neil Russack describes what would happen if you were sick and came to one of these temples. "You would lie in one of the temple baths to purify the soul, then move to the sanctuary to sleep, to incubate the vision and dream the sacred dream." We also know that they would bring gifts, make a sacrifice, pray. They trusted that their honoring of the dream that came to them, their "lying down upon it," would ensure that the dream sent by the gods and the dream's meaning would guide and heal them. This ritual dream practice began in the fifth century BCE when Sophocles dedicated the first healing shrine in Greece to Aesculapius. Eventually over 300 shrines in Greece and the Roman Empire were active until the second century CE.

One meaning of the word *incubation* is "to give form to, to allow what is unformed to form." Giving form to a dream is a process in which we are not active participants. We set this process in motion, but for the most part it is a quiet time in which we don't notice any changes. Like the cocoon in which the caterpillar undergoes metamorphosis, the dream is working its transformation unseen. One day we notice that it has changed us.

Incubation is both the easiest step in the process of transformation and the most difficult. It requires no effort or hard work, only stillness and trust. It is difficult because it asks us to wait patiently. This is the time to let go and respect our inborn rhythms of healing. We never know what causes a dream to release its meaning. So after we have worked with its imagery, we allow the process to continue without our mind's involvement. This is the winter of dreamwork, the time of the bear's hibernation—the time of deep snow and quiet waiting. It is part of the natural rhythm of the seasons: stillness followed by growth. Incubation gives the psyche a rest, especially after work with intense imagery.

What might you sense, if anything at all, during this period? When I pay attention during this phase, I am most aware of a tenderness in my heart as I cradle my dream imagery in my chest and throat. Another person may simply continue on with life, trusting in the unseen.

This process is literally an unseen one. In fact all our dreams are incubating unnoticed whenever we are not focused on them. While we go about our daily lives, they live quietly within us. As conscious dreamers, we simply make ourselves aware. We bring both our intention and attention to make this a conscious part of our dreamwork.

The Seven Sleepers Teaching

The incubation process continued for two centuries while the seven young people slept in the cave. The cave was the Sleepers' chrysalis. They did not fight the process. They chose it. They entered the cave carrying desire in their hearts. They lay down together. They had deep trust in the purpose and meaningfulness of their dreams.

The cave they slept in looked like an ordinary cave. Yet within it shone a golden light. These were no ordinary sleepers. They were the few who were willing to die for their beliefs. They were the few who heard the call to leave the world and believed that their dreaming could make a difference. Inside their chrysalis, the Sleepers surrendered their doubts and fears.

Which Dreams to Incubate

Sometimes you may sense that a dream is important because your heart is singing when you wake up. The dream, however, seems mysterious, and you are not sure what it has to do with your life. This is a dream to incubate.

When disturbing imagery from our dreams is too much with us

and we need a respite, we can incubate that imagery. Imagine wrapping such a dream in a golden cocoon (like the butterfly's chrysalis), then placing it in your heart. This can lead to the transformation of both the imagery and your feelings toward it. Remember: dark dreams are gifts that can liquefy in the Impossible Darkness, as in Kim Rosen's poem. When they emerge into the light of consciousness, they will reveal themselves. This incubation process will give you the strength to take in their truth.

Why Incubate a Dream?

This is the subtlest and most elusive stage in conscious dreamwork. Dreams need rest. If you overwork a dream, you kill its spirit. Let your practice ebb and flow with dreams, rather than continuously working hard on them. Allow nature's ongoing cycles of activity and rest to guide you. Learning when a dream needs rest is like listening to your body. Don't override its natural intelligence; let it tell you what it needs.

After I had written the story "Raette's Last Dance," I didn't know where to go with the octopus dreams. When other issues caught my attention, I let go of the octopus journey. I didn't drop the dreams into oblivion. I just stopped my active creative efforts. Then, one midnight, I awoke with a dream fragment. After recording it in my dream journal, I left it alone. It nagged me, and a week later I began a mandala with the question, "What will heal me?" After making two more mandalas, I realized I was back in the octopus story and this dream fragment was a continuation of it. *I find a box with my parts in it and want to bring these lost parts before the Divine to be healed.*

By letting the octopus imagery rest, I had received guidance for the next healing step. And that dream fragment led to its own question: "What does the Divine look like to me?" In meditation I asked for a symbol of God, then made an illuminated mandala of this symbol. With each pencil stroke, I was healing the little octopus. I knew I could now bring the torn octopus to the Divine Presence. At the time I tried to heal the octopus solely with human hands, I had no image of God that I could resonate with. Later, during the construction of my studio, I placed this mandala in the wall behind the sheetrock, to remind me that the Divine is always present, though invisible.

How to Practice Incubation

First, formulate a clear request or intention for a dream. Write it down, and then watch your dreams for a response, knowing that the dream may come in an unexpected way. In daily life, you can entrust a dream to the deep self, and wait for its meaning to be revealed.

We can incubate a single dream, an image, or a series of images. In the process of incubation we can discern six separate steps.

1. *Learn to recognize which dreams or images to incubate.*

Be selective and trust your inner knowing. Obviously you cannot go through this process with every dream, and not every dream needs such thorough work. Certain dreams and images will insist on being incubated. These are the ones that linger around the edges of your consciousness, reappearing in meditation or perhaps when you are driving down the highway. Dreams that need clarity or ones with haunting imagery are good candidates for incubation.

2. *Set your intention to incubate the dream or image.*

From the moment you begin to create around a dream, you are treating this dream as significant. You sense it carries a meaning and you want to know it. By stating your intent toward the dream, you are making your desire more conscious.

An intention can be as simple as "This dream seems significant. It holds a message I want to understand with all of me—my mind, feelings, heart, and body. I allow its wisdom the time it needs to gestate. I trust this is happening, even when I cannot see what is going on."

3. *Enter the resting stage.*

There is nothing to do in the resting stage but to let go. Let the natural processes of your self take over. Go on with the next dream and the next. When the dream you are incubating bubbles up, remember it gently. Tell yourself it is okay not to know everything about the dream at once.

4. *Wait.*

Waiting can be difficult, for it requires patience: Nothing seems to be happening. In one of my dreams, I learned that it takes prayer and patience to break the complex code that makes me an outsider. To solve this problem I must carry the numbers in the equation out "far enough," farther than my ego wants to go. Each dream has its

5. WHAT IS INCUBATION?

own complex code. We never know how deeply we will have to explore before the dream is decoded.

In his early childhood, Carl Jung had a dream that preoccupied him all his life. He recognized it as an important dream, which he could not speak about as a child. So he carried it in his memory and heart for many years, until one day he realized its meaning.

It takes trust and patience for humans to sit in the space of not knowing. Every dream has its own timing: Some caterpillars metamorphose into butterflies in ten days; others take six to eight months. The caterpillar within the cocoon instinctively goes through its process. It does not die. It is a model for us as we continue with our daily lives, trusting that transformation is happening within us.

5. *Receive what comes to you.*

When a dream is being incubated in the cave of your consciousness, you may have related dreams. Be aware of new imagery coming into your dreams that may shed light on a dream you are incubating. The imagery of each dream can be unique, and the dreams either similar or wildly dissimilar. You must find the connections.

6. *Give birth to awareness.*

Suddenly you have an insight. Something rigid has shifted inside you. You are amazed and delighted. You don't even remember the process leading to this place. Entering the unknown and having faith, you are changed.

In this place of light, no matter how tiny the change, you recognize and are grateful that you have given birth and have been transformed. You have become the butterfly, free of the cocoon. The rune *Dagaz* speaks of this process. Ralph Blum in *The Book of Runes* tells us that this rune signifies breakthrough, transformation, and day. He advises that, when you break through into the light of day, you do not "collapse yourself into the future to behave recklessly." With joy and respect for each new awareness, you will be prepared for your next dream.

Working With Resistance

Distrusting Inactivity

We live in a culture in the thrall of activity and its contemporary companion, anxiety. We grow up learning to place an inordinate value on results. Society gives little praise and attention to the gestating stages of any creative act, but all artists and scientists know the value of these stages. They know there is a time when you cannot push, when you must let go. This is a hard stage to accept if you are attached to activity and end-results.

In this stage you trust and surrender, but you are not helpless. Surrender calls for faith that there are forces in the universe guiding our evolution. If we do not surrender our will, which wants to be in charge, the process of transformation is unlikely to be completed.

Dreamwork is both active and receptive. In the incubation stage you "lie down upon" the image or dream so that you can receive the benefits of the deeper kavannah working with the dream. The active part is your decision about what and when to engage in incubation. In the process of working with a dream a receptive *doing* follows an active *doing*, and the process continues in a rhythmic cycle of activity and rest, just as sleep follows wakefulness. Vigorous activity is not what sustains the world. The rhythm of activity and receptivity does.

Fighting Against the Unknown

When we take a dark dream into our hearts and allow it to incubate, we don't know how it will affect us. We cannot *will* the effect it will have on us. We may think we have sunk into the darkness of the dream, but only a part of us needs to sink. Another part of us can remain on firm ground, waiting and watching. There is an ancient Sumerian tale that shows the way to enter the unknown of the incubation process. In this myth Inanna, Queen of Heaven, willingly journeys to the underworld to meet her dark sister Ereshkigal. Sylvia Brinton Perera in *Descent to the Goddess* says that before Inanna left heaven, she instructed her "trusted female executive" Ninshubur to send help if she did not emerge in three days. When Inanna arrived in the underworld, she was made to hang in a deathlike stasis. When she did not return, Ninshubur pleaded with the gods for help. Finally two little mourners, small enough to enter unseen, were sent to the underworld to rescue Inanna. Through their compassionate efforts Inanna was restored to life. Drawing an analogy to dreamwork, Ninshubur is the ego that stays connected to the upper world of waking consciousness.

We can rescue and restore submerged parts of ourselves with a healthy ego. With that essential grounding, we can allow a part of us to descend into the dark imagery of our nightmares, to mourn and reunite with the lost parts of ourselves.

5. WHAT IS INCUBATION?

A Conscious Dreamer: Amanda

Amanda is a full-time mother and graphic artist, who trusts the power of her dream imagery and its ability to transform her. She works creatively with her strongest dreams, though she has many dreams to choose from. She often lets those dreams choose themselves, allowing two or three dreams to guide her at once. In this way she slows the process, while her dreams naturally incubate.

Amanda worked for a year with three dreams that seemed related to each other. "The first dream was about a whale, a dream like a vision. I kept it with me as a guiding light throughout the year. *A mother whale and her young calf are diving in the ocean, down to the bottom and rising to the surface to breach. They are doing this over and over again with great joy.*

"This was a very powerful dream. I was curious to discover the significance of whales in my unconscious life, so I had a dialogue with the larger whale. I wrote down my questions with my right hand and answered with my left.

Amanda: Whale woman, come and speak to me. Why did you come and visit me in my dream?

Whale: Because I love you. I am your mother.

Amanda: What can you teach me, mother?

Whale: I can teach you your woman wisdom.

Amanda: How can I grow up?

Whale: You are grown up. You have the purity and essence of woman in your heart. I am teaching you to swim in your tears with joy and to rise like the sun over the water, and to breech, bearing your weight like a child. Show your gigantic splash to the world; let it show them peace. You will swim to the very bottom, experience the darkness, and in splendor, rise up over and over again. Each time you will sing a song of the woman/whale.

Amanda: Am I alone?

Whale: No, your tears are part of a vast ocean. The rocks at the bottom are your friends and they comfort you. The sun helps you shine. You will always be wet.

Amanda: Where will I go?

Whale: You will go with God.

That dialogue gave Amanda the courage to go into the scary places of her dark emotions. "I would go to the bottom and come up. As a result, I started to be able to create. It gave me courage to experience my emotions, to draw and create, make them concrete and show them to the world. The whale really helped me begin to understand myself as a woman."

When Amanda was a young girl, her parents would dress her up and make her appear before their company. "I was the pretty one and I grew up being the beautiful, sexy one. My mother was very beautiful, also. My father had a fast, furious, and unpredictable temper, often aimed toward my mother and me because I looked like my mother.

"So I turned my sexuality off. I made a conscious decision to be a boy. I hung around guys. I became very competitive and tough—without feelings. I saw women as victims. If you were a woman, you were manipulative, sexy, and evil. Then when I was sixteen, I was kidnapped and raped by two men. After that I really shut down. When I was seventeen, I got pregnant from a boyfriend. I wandered around,

5. WHAT IS INCUBATION?

not knowing what to do. I came back home and I was four months pregnant. My father grabbed my stomach, twisted it and said, 'You're getting fat.' I had a miscarriage. I believed he had murdered my child. I was really dead, walking around numb.

"When I was twenty-eight, I married a gentle man and started having children. But I had a lot of confusion. Unconsciously, I was still very male. I didn't want to let go of that busy, working person who didn't have to be a gentle, kind, and nurturing woman. I was trying to breast-feed and be caring, and my husband was trying to care for me. It was scary to let go. I had terrible insomnia. Sometimes I wouldn't sleep for three or four nights at a time. In addition to mothering, I was working freelance as a graphic artist. It was stressful because I wanted everyone's role—my husband's, my child's, and mine. I was running on sheer will power.

"By the time I had the whale dream, I had birthed my two children. I had started bodywork and therapy. With one child, I could straddle two worlds. With two it was impossible. I had to surrender to motherhood. I stayed home and let my husband earn our income. I was terrified of sex, especially as I became more in touch with my emotions. Before, I was not there, just dead.

"The whale dream came in the spring. I titled it 'The Song of the Whale.' The feeling of water in the dream fits me. I love to float in the water and dive. Water symbolizes emotion, femininity, and tears to me. Knowing I have all that pain and all those tears makes me what I am. It's okay to have all those tears and to swim in them and discover who you are in them."

Amanda's next strong dream took place in a pit, where a

demolished house had fallen. Amanda knew there was something evil down in the pit, which she could not bear to look at. She kept falling into it and scrambling up again, then slipping down in a mini-landslide. This happened several times. Finally she woke up, terrified and crying. She lay awake for about ten minutes, and then she went back to sleep and into the dream.

"I am sitting at the top of the pit. There is a beautiful blonde woman in the pit, sitting on top of the house ruins. I hadn't seen her before. I look at her and know she is intrinsically evil. I am petrified of her, but I make the decision to face her. I slide into the pit to look at her, but when I get to the bottom she is gone. I wake up with a sense of triumph.

"When I was growing up my grandmother, who used to tell me I was a wicked little thing, had dyed platinum blonde hair. She wore leopard-skin outfits all the time. We used to call her Diamond Lil because she played cards and drank a lot. I grew up believing that beautiful blonde women incite men to commit acts of violence against them.

Amanda cultivated her relationship with women to try and understand them. She joined a woman's "moon lodge" and began working with totem animals in her dreams.

"I made a conscious decision to let myself experience my emotions, to go deeply into my soul and look at who I am. I need to create to understand who I am.

"For several months this scraggly gray wolf—mean, angry and half-starved—had been present in my dreams. I dreamed *I was a young girl about ten or twelve years old, and I was battling this wolf. He wanted to bite my head off, so the battle raged on until finally I subdued him and covered his mouth with a red muzzle. I spoke to him gently*

5. WHAT IS INCUBATION?

and began to feel a great love and acceptance towards him. I told him this, and took his great head into my hands. He transformed. He became a luxuriant, beautiful, alpha male wolf. He told me his name, which was Akai-Shee. A great joy surged through me, and a great love for this creature, who is my child that was denied. I removed his muzzle, and he began to battle the other wolves that surrounded us. He won, always, and climbed a hill to howl in ecstasy.

I woke up with a sense of combat and a feeling of joy. The joy stayed with me. The emotion I experienced in facing the wolf was stronger and purer and deeper than I had ever experienced.

"As I thought about the whale and the wolf, I realized the whale is my feminine and the wolf is my masculine. The wolf dream was balancing my male and female. When I used to draw and paint and create, I was still a *doer*. My art didn't seem to touch the real me. I was into getting it done. The whale and wolf dreams helped me to go deeper. Now my art is much more truthful. It is really Amanda who is coming out.

"All my dream imagery is coming out in my art. I have drawn more pictures and written more stories this year than ever in my life. I want to create and create, though I have less time, but time isn't an issue. These things just bubble out so easily now.

"I wrote three stories this year that chart my process of self-discovery. They are all fables. As a girl, I missed celebrating those rites of passage, like when you have your first period and you discover your sexuality. With those stories I am giving myself my own rites of passage. One is about a girl in a tower. Another is about a girl falling into a dark hole. They are very simple.

"I drew a totem pole of a woman whose chin rests on her hand, her hand merges into a whale's tail, the whale goes into a wolf's head, which goes into another animal, and on up the pole.

"I didn't realize how exciting dreams could be. In the past, I read so many books trying to find out who I am, but I found I couldn't be wise in myself until I dove into myself.

"These three dreams were mythic and powerful. Having cherished them this year, I feel much more comfortable being a woman, and in finding out who I am. I know now I can swim down to the bottom and come back up again. I know I'm not going to stay in the bottom, trapped.

"When I feel like the whale, the course seems much clearer than when I try to figure out who Amanda is and what she wants to do. When I am a whale, I just dive and surface and dive again. Before I was only my mind."'

6

Creating a Dream Collection

Last night, as I was sleeping,
I dreamt—marvellous error!—
that a spring was breaking
out in my heart.
I said: Along which secret aqueduct,
Oh water, are you coming to me,
water of a new life
that I have never drunk?

Last night, as I was sleeping,
I dreamt—marvellous error!—
that I had a beehive
here inside my heart.
And the golden bees
were making white combs
and sweet honey
from my old failures.

Last night, as I was sleeping,
I dreamt—marvellous error!—
that a fiery sun was giving
light inside my heart.
It was fiery because I felt
warmth as from a hearth,
and sun because it gave light
and brought tears to my eyes.

Last night, as I slept,
I dreamt—marvellous error!—

> that it was God I had
> here inside my heart.
>
> —Antonio Machado
> *Translated by Robert Bly*

A Panorama of Dreams

A single dream can stand alone, reflecting one vista. A series of dreams reveals a panorama. Antonio Machado dreams that inside his heart, he has a "spring breaking out;" then a beehive with "golden bees... making white combs and sweet honey" from his failures; then a fiery sun giving its light and warmth, bringing tears to the poet's eyes. At last, he recognizes that it is simply God in his heart. As individual dream images they do not truly describe the Divine, but collectively they surprise us, so we come away from the poem with a recognition of the inexpressible. In the same way dreams yield surprising insights when we look at them in relationship with one another.

When you first start dreamwork, it is essential to practice with individual dreams. Trying to understand multiple dreams is confusing at the beginning, but insight will come with experience. When you work with a group of dreams, you can use the same tools I recommend for working with individual dreams.

A group of resonant dreams reveals the changes you are undergoing, the deepening of your awareness, the way you are handling your issues, and any persistent resistance. If you have any doubts about your soul's desire, look for a frequent theme in your dreams. Your soul conveys the same message ten thousand ways. A collection of dreams is like a crystal with many facets. Looking into any facet, you see the center of the gem. Looking at the whole gem, you see its deeper beauty. It is like being inside its heart. Assembling a dream collection is an active part of the process of creating yourself whole.

Finding a Thread of Connection Between Dreams

I first explored dream collections with one of my dream groups. After months of work with single dreams, the dreamers began to make spontaneous connections between their dreams. So I focused their work on the thread of connection that ran through multiple dreams. This helped them to see their recurrent messages more clearly and to experience their dreams wholistically.

Each dreamer came to this session with a minimum of five recent dreams. First, I led them in a meditation to open their intuitive minds and to find the common thread running through their dream collection. To add another dimension to their search, they intuitively selected one of Strephon Kaplan-Williams' archetypal Dream Cards. (Kaplan-Williams has designed a compendium of over 5,000 dream and life symbols, based on his study of about 10,000 dreams.) I have used this deck as an adjunct to my dream imagery, trusting in synchronicity when I draw a card it. Another resource of this kind is Deborah Koff-Chapin's Soul Cards.

From this collected raw material each dreamer then created poems, artwork, dramatic or musical pieces, and shared them with the group. If dreamers were confused or needed help, I led them deeper into their artistic material to find the intuitive voice that would reveal the next step or missing piece.

I find it invaluable to explore groups of my dreams. When I entered menopause, I honored my dream voice by writing and illustrating a personal book. I was aware that my way of being as a woman was dissolving. I realized I needed to create a passage for myself, a closure of the past and an opening to the future. I searched my most recent dreams, jotting down phrases that jumped out at me. Then I looked for a story line. I discovered it began with my birth and included the distorted lenses through which I had viewed the world. It included harm done to my sensitive soul by the adults around me who had their own distortions. All of this I was surrendering, dissolving, and leaving behind as I passed into older adulthood. Menopause named the physical changes, but I was undertaking a spiritual change. I called my book *Becoming Transparent*. Writing and illustrating it has helped me see the deeper shift that was occurring. It gave me a better understanding of the physical, emotional and spiritual changes that come with menopause. With it came the glimmer of a new beginning.

The Seven Sleepers Teaching

One sleeper, hidden alone in the mountains, saying his own prayers, could have dreamed himself whole. But could his dreams have manifested the transformation that occurred in his land? The legend of the Seven Sleepers speaks to the power and knowledge of many dreams. These dreams clustered themselves into a story that fed the hearts of

6. CREATING A DREAM COLLECTION

listeners for hundreds of years after. It makes dreamers like us realize that we are no different than the original seven.

If I consider the legend as a dream, each of the Sleepers becomes an aspect of me. If the dreamers each have a different version of my soul's core story, seeing the connections between them makes my story clearer and more poignant. I trust the truth of my inner story. I trace the etchings of its meaning deeper and deeper, comforted by an unseen wisdom. I know that beside me are all the dreams of the greater community of dreamers. I am not wandering through life alone. Like the Sleepers who trusted in their long sleep, I awaken each day to the opportunity of knowing more about my connection to both humanity and Spirit. Whenever I feel lost, I remember that one dream lies down next to another dream; clustered together, they illuminate the darkness.

How to Create a Collection

As you go through these steps you will notice that each dream is a kind of shorthand that records part of the bigger soul message.

- Periodically reread the dreams recorded in your journal.
- Highlight significant images and phrases and title your dreams if you haven't already done so.
- Jot down images that reappear.
- Look for themes, characters and symbols that repeat themselves.

Gathering a collection of dreams is similar to making a friendship or theme quilt, where many quilters design individual squares, each one a different variation on the theme. Each square is a unique design but is not a quilt in itself. The squares must be laid in front of the quilter, who searches for the best composition. As she places them in different combinations, she begins to see connections between the squares. When the design has a harmonious look, the pieces are sewn together and the finished quilt reveals its theme. In a sense, we are making friends with ourselves when we piece together our own imagery.

I have been exploring dream series for years, and I am still startled by the distinct weave that runs through them. Again and again I feel a surge of joy and relief at finding a thread of connection in my internal world. It is like discovering a clear path through the dark woods when you thought you were lost. Many people consult psychics and astrologers to find the same path. Wise ones can be helpful, but when you learn to consult your dreams, you will discover your own oracle within.

Eva Pierrakos, in one of the Pathwork [a spiritual teaching and discipline] lectures, talked about the wellspring of love and knowledge that resides deep within us. "Within each individual there exists a well of wisdom and love. There is a treasure deep within you which can come to the fore only as you become aware of all those aspects of yourself that bar access to this treasure. You are accustomed to look for truth, guidance, and solutions to your problems outside yourself—perhaps through wise teachings, through a helping hand, or even for guidance that comes from outside yourself. But the most reliable and realistic answers come from within. In order to tap that well, outside help is necessary, but it is valuable only if it finally succeeds in bringing you to this inner well." (*Three Aspects that Prevent Loving*)

The theme of a series of dreams may be overt, or may be buried so that you must search for it. You may want to explore your cryptic dreams with a skilled dreamer. You do have the answers inside you and the ability to illuminate the connections; however, your fear of revelation or change may prevent you from discovering your knowing. This work invites you to practice seeing below the surface.

Transforming a Series of Dreams Into Creative Expression

There are many ways to create from your dream series. Collage and dream poetry lend themselves to this kind of work, as does performance art. Select one of these art forms to enrich your dreamwork:

Collage

To make a collage with a series of dreams you will need a large sheet of poster board or heavy white cardboard, glue, and scissors. First review the dreams you want to include. Make a list of images, colors, and shapes. Then look for representations in magazines, catalogs, old greeting cards, wrapping paper, yarn, and so on. You may want to draw or paint some images, cutting them from beautiful colored papers.

There is no right or wrong way to make a collage. Experiment. Lay your materials around you. Then put on music, light a candle and sit quietly to listen for your intention. Write this intention on the back of the paper. Then lay the images on the paper, trying out various positions, letting your intuition and feelings guide you. The final layout will reveal something about your dream path at that moment. Let the collage become a new dream.

Leave an hour or two to work on it. Find a space where you can leave it out, if you cannot finish it in one sitting. When you come back, look at it all again before gluing everything in place. Reread your intention and then title and date it. Hang your collage in a special place so you can see it frequently. Observe which images lie side by side, and which are farthest apart. Let their placement and relative sizes speak to you. Each time you look at the collage, notice any new realizations. Jot down these insights and inspirations. Your collage may move you to write a poem: let it.

Story

Write a story from your imagery; then add drawings or pictures. When you weave disparate dream imagery into a story, meanings hidden within individual dreams may suddenly pop into view. You might dream, for example, of your friend riding her bicycle and carrying her pet pig in her arms. Each of these symbols (friend, bicycle, and pet pig) is an aspect of you. They offer insight into your personal nature that you might not otherwise see so readily. Perhaps this dream says something about "carrying and caring," about your iconoclastic nature, or about your ability to love what society disdains. The story

6. CREATING A DREAM COLLECTION

you write should come out of your personal associations to each character or symbol in the dream.

The story of your dreams can be simple or complex. One dreamer creates small books that read like a collection of poetry, illuminated with watercolor pictures of her dream images. My menopause passage book, *Becoming Transparent*, began as a simple poetic story, and grew until it was four chapters long. It began with my physical birth and ended with my spiritual birth, the emergence of my creativity. Since I intended it as a gift to myself, I used a beautiful hardbound book, sturdy enough to be handled over the many months it would take to do the illustrations. I searched my dream journals to select imagery that helped to tell the story of my interior life. I chose not to embellish the story, but to let my dream imagery speak for itself. Since this was a private story, it didn't matter to me if my dream quotes made sense to anyone else. Thus I wrote lines like, "her mother had empty breasts;" a line I found humorous, "She found a fireman who promised to fill her hole with his hose, but her pond had a hidden leak;" and the mysterious image of Itzhak Perlman's daughter keeping her breasts bound in a slim mink bra, beneath her mink suit, her baby's eyes coated and "her pockets were full of other people's jokes."

Since this book also represented my creative play, I experimented with a variety of art media as I illustrated it, using oil pastels, colored pencils, watercolors, pen and ink, and collage. In the next book I want to choose one medium for all of the illustrations.

Touch Drawing

Touch Drawing is a simple, primal process of painting with your hands. Developed by Deborah Koff-Chapin, this visual mapping lends itself to working with one dream or a series. No artistic training or experience is necessary to engage in this evocative and integrative process. Basically, you ink a drawing board with washable oil paints on a board, roll them smooth, then lay a sheet of paper over that and begin to draw, using your hands and fingers, staying attuned to your feelings, emotional and physical. There are many variations to this process, but the two most important parts are staying true to what is going on internally in each moment and allowing yourself to make multiple paintings in one sitting, which usually lasts 60-90 minutes.

Touch Drawing has the qualities of a dream. Images appear very quickly, similar to the dream state. They appear, disappear, change, and reappear. They are like dreams, creating momentum as new variations arise. Transformation happens as you surrender to the images that emerge under the pressure of your hands, fingers, and nails and allow your soul to express the inner landscape.

Making these drawings is like making dreams. Stepping back from them and witnessing the whole assemblage gives you the same perspective as being witness to a series of dreams. As you look at each one, you can give it a quick title. In the end you have a poetic description of your now-visible transformation. This is an accessible process for everyone which Deborah Koff-Chapin demonstrates in a video called *Through the Veil: The Story of Touch Drawing.* She also has written a handbook called *Drawing Out Your Soul: The Touch*

Drawing Handbook. However, she recommends that the process is best seen and experienced with a facilitator before doing it on your own.

Learning From a Collection

The desire for clear consciousness is also a desire to heal the spirit. Once you have found the connecting threads between your dreams and honored them through creative expression, it is time to be witness to your process. This review is an ongoing practice. I encourage you to meet yourself completely, with reverence and respect.

After I wrote *Becoming Transparent*, I began to realize what the dreams and the process of making the book meant to me. Like a wedding or graduation scrapbook, this book became a means of remembering myself with all my wounds and graces. It allowed me to integrate the experience of this essential period of my life. The passage through midlife becomes a crisis when and where we are unconscious about what is happening. I wanted to be as aware as possible, to pick up missing threads from my life. Edward Hoffman, a clinical psychologist who has written about Jewish mysticism and psychology, describes one of the keys of Kabbalistic dreamwork as letting "your dreams be a pathway to high consciousness." Searching my dreams helped me see what spiritual transitions I was making while my body was making its hormonal passage.

Working With Resistance

You may think working with a group of dreams is too much work. It does take a commitment of time and energy to create a book of dreams. You might only make one collection of dreams in your lifetime, but that collection can deeply affect you. You are your dreams. As you search and weave your dream imagery into a new design, you are rediscovering yourself. If a large collection is too much to undertake, choose to create a small collection of three or four dreams on a theme. Instead of making a book, you could make a string of prayer flags, one for each dream.

When we study our dreams over time, we are able to see the recurring patterns and develop an appreciation for the intricacies of dream messages. We can see the dreams and their many meanings holographically. We may also see what our karmic issues are. We may perceive that our patterns of behavior are the result of many repeated actions and that creating new patterns is equally slow. The soul's knowledge penetrates our awareness gradually. It may need to make many attempts to bypass our ingrained defenses to affect real change. Create a collection of dreams if only to see the persistence of your soul. The result may surprise you.

6. CREATING A DREAM COLLECTION

A Conscious Dreamer: Ingrid

Ingrid collected her dreams for ten to fifteen years before she joined my women's dream group. She had even used them in her graduate thesis about her grief work around her mother, called Journey into the Dark. Ingrid says, "My dreams are one way my higher self communicates with me. Being in a regular dream group made me more alert to my dreams."

While this group was meeting, Ingrid had several dreams on a similar theme. Her exploration of them enabled her to have a clear overview of the changes she was making in her life and to experience the emotional support of these dreams. In each of them she was on a roof with no easy way to get down. A fourth dream, directly related to these, appeared several months later. At the time of these dreams, she was building a private practice as a psychotherapist, having left a full-time job in a hospital the year before. Things were going well, but suddenly she lost two of her consulting contracts at the same time. She was strongly opposed to returning to a hospital job, so she decided to live partly on her savings and to continue building her practice. But she was having a lot of anxiety based on her feelings of financial insecurity.

"I felt like I was doing a high-wire act. The crisis was at its height. When I started contemplating taking a full-time job in a clinic, I began having these dreams. In each one there is the metaphor of being on a roof with nothing to hang on to. I am slipping and sliding and afraid I am going to fall. I am very frightened. I have no way to get down except by jumping or falling. I am afraid I will get hurt."

Dream #1: *Together with another woman, I am spying on the secrets of a power plant. We have to climb on the roof so we can see the mechanism that makes it work. We see a flowing waterfall and know that the secret is the flowing. When we want to go back, we have to cross a roof that is very steep. It's not easy to keep our balance. From the edge of the roof we have to jump down about fifteen feet. We know that if we curl together, we will come down safely. The other woman goes first. She tells me to close my eyes because the body knows what it has to do.*

Dream #2: *I meet a young man and we fall in love. He smuggles me into the dorm where he lives. We must be careful that nobody sees me because he's not allowed to bring women into the dorm. While I am there, he has to leave and I'm alone in his room. I'm curious about the dorm and leave his room while he is gone. Unfortunately, someone sees me, and people get suspicious. Suddenly my friend is back and we have to flee. The only way we can go is upstairs, which leads to an attic with a skylight. We climb up the skylight; he goes first. While I am still climbing, I see him lose his hold on the roof and start to slide down. I wonder if the gutter will stop him, because the roof is very steep. No matter what, I know I have to follow him.*

In Ingrid's journal she writes, "This is my second steep roof dream in which I know eventually I will fall down or have to jump down. There simply is no other way. It probably is going to be all right. What is the steep roof in my life? Is it my precarious financial situation? What does falling down or jumping down mean? It has a quality of jumping into an abyss. I connect that with giving up false beliefs and allowing for the possibility that what I consider dangerous might not be that dangerous after all."

6. CREATING A DREAM COLLECTION

Ingrid shared each of these dreams with the group. She chose to work with the second dream by reentering it and extending it. This time she discovered the steep roof led to a lower roof, which led to an even lower roof; eventually she was able to climb down to the ground safely. The dream that followed showed that her attitude toward her situation was beginning to change.

Dream #3: *I am in Berlin, walking through the city with my friend. We are going through an old historic park with the remains of a castle. After a while we don't know where we are, so my friend goes to get a map. She is gone for a long time and doesn't come back. In looking for her, I go onto the roof of the castle, which is not that high. I slide down one side, where the roof goes down like a slide. I'm having fun. Later on I meet my friend again.*

"Clearly I had become playful in my dream state. These dreams helped me to have more trust—to hang in there and not compromise by finding a full-time job, which was not what I wanted to do anymore. I wanted more flexibility to continue my work fostering a dialogue between Germans and Jews in the United States and between those in Germany and Israel. So I worked with these dreams—writing, thinking about them, sharing them with others, and expanding them. As I talked about them, I began to see the progression. Later that year, I dislocated my elbow and sprained my ankle. Looking back at the first dream, I understood that these accidents happened where I wasn't flowing. These accidents grounded me and taught me what the woman in the first dream had said, that 'the body knows what it has to do.' By the end of the year I realized these dreams were about inner and outer grounding. I began doing a grounding exercise every morning and accepting that my body has a lot of wisdom I wasn't hearing."

Soon after, Ingrid had a dream that clearly was related to the others.

Dream #4: *I'm on a very high mountain that has a platform on top. I can get back by walking down a very steep trail or with a helicopter. I am scared of both and it makes me dizzy. Then I realize there is a third possibility. On the inside of the mountain there is a cable car which goes down slowly and safely. I'm relieved and go down without any problem.*

"One part of me always knew it wasn't right to go back to working in an institution full-time. Yet the other side had doubts. I wasn't actively aware of praying or asking for dream guidance because I had an underlying sense of knowing what I needed to do. These dreams helped me to deal with ongoing insecurity and panic. They helped me develop a new attitude. I knew my intention was clear. I was ready to see what the truth was for me. I would accept what was right.

"Once I was less panicked about my finances, the outer situation changed. A few months later I was able to pay for my ticket to Israel for the German/Jewish group meeting.

"Now I don't know what is going to happen, but my dreams have shifted to my waking life. Last week in Israel I found myself going high up a mountain in Sinai, Mount Moses, climbing in the dark, then watching the sunrise. It was a profound experience for me. I have always been afraid of heights. Walking this mountain, I was not afraid. It was okay, even though it was pretty steep at times. It was a pilgrimage. It was the first thing I did in the New Year, and it was very significant to me. For years I had wanted to do this.

6. CREATING A DREAM COLLECTION

"I'm still figuring out the meaning of this pilgrimage, and I'm still going through this change in my career. But now I'm so full of this pilgrimage that I'm not worried. I've learned to trust. Being up on the mountain made a lot of other things insignificant."

7

Connecting With Other Conscious Dreamers

> The soul of this community is coming
> toward us, the sun on his forehead . . .
>
> Don't ruin this chance with
> politeness and easy promises. The
> help we called for is here, the
> invitation to join with great souls.
>
> —Rumi
> *Translated by Coleman Barks*

The Dream Community

Dreams call us to community. They invite us to join with other great souls. When you make a commitment to be a conscious dreamer, you want to connect with other conscious dreamers. By doing this you will discover your place in the community of dreamers. Humans seek connection with others mentally, physically, emotionally, and spiritually.

Dreams are individual and personal; they are also universal and communal. We can be blind to the meaning of our own dreams, but as soon as we share them their meaning begins to emerge. Early in my dreamwork I discovered a small gem, a book called *Awakening: A*

7. CONNECTING WITH OTHER CONSCIOUS DREAMERS

Dream Journal, by Ellen Foreman. She has this to say about dream community:

> "Dream language draws upon archetypal and cultural references, such as myths, fairy tales, and folk tales, as well as on movies, music, and art that are shared by many people in a society. Sharing your dreams with others is an astounding experience because images that you thought private or obscure often strike common chords in others. Another person's intuitive response to your dream image can greatly enrich your insights into your own dream."

No matter what calls you to commune with other dreamers, this phase of dreamwork is inevitable. Even when we feel hermit-like, our dreams are filled with others.

What is a community of dreamers? Two or more people who come together to hold one another's dreams. A community may be led by an accomplished dreamer. It may be a leaderless group. It may be family or friends. There were years when I was part of a dream community led by a teacher; now I am a dream teacher. I have always shared dreams with my husband, and listened to my children's dreams. My community is made up of all the dreamers who come to me for help with their dreams, as well as my close friends with whom I share my dreams and dream art. I am connected to each dreamer who shared the story of his or her dreams for this book. I am connected to each dreamer who has been to one of my workshops. I feel a connection to all dreamers who honor their dreams.

The Seven Sleepers Teaching

The Seven Sleepers dreamed in community and devoted their long sleep to dreaming together. I imagine *them struggling like any community but committed to a common goal. They listen to one another. As each dreamer's images arise and are digested, they connect with the images of their fellow dreamers. They appreciate the wisdom of one another's dreams. They learn from each other's dreams. They know that dreams speak to all of humanity and seek the best for us. The Seven Sleepers know that the soul has the power to dream its way to God. They listen to one another and wed their passions to the transformative dream.*

Community Dream Models

A popular model of the dream community in the 1960s and 70s was that of the Senoi, a tribe living in the mountainous jungles of Malaysia. These people, who were reputed to be free from neuroses or mental illness, had learned to guide their communal lives by their dreams. Though this description of the Senoi has been debunked by some scholars, it is appreciated by many dreamers as an ideal to work towards.

Many dream community models have come from other native peoples. For example, in the early 1960s Dr. Robert Van de Castle studied the Cuna Indians on the San Blas Islands off the Atlantic coast of Panama. In *Our Dreaming Mind* he wrote, "If someone had what was considered an important dream, there would be no hesitation to report it at a town council meeting." If that dream contained an

7. CONNECTING WITH OTHER CONSCIOUS DREAMERS

ominous reference with a personal threat, then action was taken to avert it, even if it meant altering the day's work plan. The Cunas taught Dr. Van de Castle "that dreams could play a central role in societal functioning: their messages were heard and shared collectively and the warnings they contained were heeded."

In *The Lucid Dreamer,* Malcolm Godwin says that, "In varying degrees all Native American tribes held the dream to be central to life itself, and the very source and foundation of all matters of the spirit." This included the power dream sought in the vision quest and the dreams that gave the tribe its "songs, dances, cures, and the designs of the complex sand paintings." Dreams were such a natural part of the culture that dances and rituals involving the use of dream-inducing herbs were created to manifest powerful dreams.

Godwin quotes a Jesuit priest who lived with the Huron tribe. "They hold nothing so precious that they would not readily deprive themselves of it for the sake of a dream. It prescribes their feasts, their dances, their songs, their games—in a word, the dream does everything and is in truth the principal God of the Hurons."

Patricia Garfield describes dreams as being such an integral part of early Native American society that people were encouraged to dream "cultural pattern dreams" for their tribes. Over time, as they were exposed to European culture, this dream practice disappeared and their dreams became focused on personal issues.

Looking backward at cultures like the Native American gives us a vision of how dreams can serve a community. How can we adapt that vision to contemporary life? As technology expands, so do the opportunities to form dream communities. No longer are we confined to physical locale or to homogenous culture. Not only do we have rapid mail systems, telephones, cell phones, rapid transit, we now have cyberspace—all of which have increased our opportunities to share our dreams.

Robert Bosnak, president of the Association for the Study of Dreams, envisions the study of dreams across many cultures because "dreaming provides a common experience known to every human on the face of the earth." Now dream community can be conducted in cyberspace. For example, he and Jill Fischer developed a global dream community in 1997 with participants in five continents. On this Internet voice program participants work with each other's dreams in real time. In *Dreamtime*, a publication of the Association for the Study of Dreams, Bosnak describes the importance of "dreamers from all cultures [having] a forum to communicate about such fundamental emotional states as encountered in the depth of dreaming... [It is also] quite useful for people from cultures in conflict... to hear each other's dreams and feel into one another through dreaming... It is hard to be prejudiced against a group you have seen at dreaming, unless of course the outside circumstances are well beyond such interventions."

What a community or culture believes about dreams greatly affects the dreams of its members. When a culture believes that dreams are important enough to guide it, dreamers will produce dreams of vision for the community. When a culture does not rely on dreams as a communal source of knowing, dreams may be seen as frivolous, or merely personal revelations.

I experienced firsthand a community's rejection of dreams as a source of guidance. My husband and I were part of a spiritual/

7. CONNECTING WITH OTHER CONSCIOUS DREAMERS

process-oriented community for many years. At the time of this event the community was wrestling with its future, moving in what I perceived as a narrower, less inclusive direction. Eventually, as a result of its decisions, a number of highly creative people left, and the community went through a difficult crisis. Before all that happened, I had several dreams that clearly pointed to the impending crisis.

In one dream *there was a fire on the center roof, which had been smoldering all day. At first I ignored it, but as the men in our community bring pails of water to put it out, I start packing our irreplaceable things to carry to safety. It takes some time to get my husband's attention and make him believe it is serious, but at last he comes around. Then the phone rings and it's a religious call.* (This community was about to have a meeting to call for a new spiritual leader.) *I tell the man calling that I can't handle this right now because we have a fire and need to call the fire department. While the men in the community are trying to call the fire department, I find my wedding dress,* (my husband and I had our wedding at this community center) *which I add to all the other sentimental things. I can always replace the basics, but my husband and I are preparing in case the whole house goes up in flames.* This dream spoke clearly about specific events occurring in the community: what was demanding its immediate attention and what action I needed to take.

When I shared my dreams with the community leaders, they told me they believed these dreams were about my personal issues. They did not see them as a serious contribution to the community. I listened to these dreams; I saw how they corroborated what was happening around us. My husband and I decided to leave the community before we were exhausted by a conflict flaring out of control.

In the Western world most people see dreams as personal, rather than communal. Hopefully, as more individuals form dream communities, communal dreaming will be appreciated and respected.

Working With Resistance

Exposing Your Intimate Self to Others

Sharing dreams with others is intimate. The dream reveals what we hide from ourselves and from each other. We all have parts we want others to see, and parts we are ashamed of and disown. The soul does not turn away from any part of us. The soul transmits everything from our darkest aspects to our most divine. Recently, I dreamed that *a young man's crime was discovered when he told his dream to a dream group. I wondered why anyone hiding a crime would work on his dreams in front of others.* Those who resist intimacy and want to stay hidden will find group dreamwork a challenge. Go slowly if you are one of those. Accept your resistance and don't try to charge through it. You don't want to reinforce it. I suggest you begin with small risks. Build a level of trust with the other members by first offering the dreams you are most comfortable with. Jump in with a riskier dream when you are ready.

7. CONNECTING WITH OTHER CONSCIOUS DREAMERS

Handling Personality Conflicts

Many yearn for community but then discover that, as in marriage, you and others have different views over such things as toothpaste, dirty socks, and care of the children. Living close to each other we find one another's wounds and blind spots. Even with a common purpose some dreamers will go through difficult interactions with one another at some time. Wise members of the group can counsel those who create conflict or distraction so that everyone can stay attuned to the power of the dreamwork.

A dream community that has established trust among its members can seek guidance in dreams for its interpersonal conflicts. Guidance should not be given to the group in a definitive way; it should be shared as an offering for the group to explore. If these dreams are not available, or the group cannot move through a stuck place, a counselor skilled in group dynamics can help.

Difficulties among adult members of dream communities usually arise when childhood wounds are re-opened. We see and react to the world from our singular perspectives, according to the beliefs about life we formed as children. When we come together to share dreams, we are able to see each other below the surface of our idealized selves. Dreams reveal our inner struggles. Listening to the dreams of someone who bothers you can open the door to communication and show you in what way you are like the person you are pushing away.

In a community of conscious dreamers each dreamer is responsible for his or her own issues and projections upon others in the community. When the community agrees to this and believes in the truth of the dream, their communal dreamwork can age like a good wine.

Unexpected Blessings

Dreams, like adventures, affect parts of your life you were not consciously addressing. Lynne's self-confidence increased dramatically after being actively involved in a dream community for a couple of years.

"Now I trust both my not-knowing and speaking what I do see. When I started studying to be a healer at the Barbara Brennan School of Healing, I believed that I couldn't see clairvoyantly and I judged this. When I was in a practice healing session and I encountered something I didn't understand, I felt scared. By the time I graduated, I had grown competent, but I still needed outside validation. The experience of reentering a dream with Raechel in the dream group and having it fully accepted without question calmed my anxiety. Being able to continue the dream imaginally showed me I can have my own knowing, and it is perfectly natural. My confidence in my intuition and my own experience has skyrocketed. It doesn't matter now if people don't hear me. I can allow whatever is happening to happen.

"I hadn't trusted myself because in my childhood, whenever I spoke the adults would say, 'That isn't true' or 'You don't mean that.' My parents and siblings have always censored me. I lived as one of my dreams described, 'Marching through enemy lines, undetected.'

"Community dreamwork has also stretched my ability to hold dreams. I had never worked with dreams before. I was looking for a process group when I was introduced to Raechel's group. Then because this was a dream group, I wanted to have dreams to share, so I had to make the effort to capture them. This effort helped me bridge the waking and dream worlds. Now I can go into dream space while I am awake. I just dial the dream frequency by sensing a vibration that comes through my crown chakra. I have learned to call for a semi-waking dream about an issue that needs more clarity and then to dialogue with the dream to gain further insight."

Creating a Dream Community

Community is formed from the same root as the words *common, communal, communion,* and *communicates.* The root connotes similarity or likeness, interdependence, sharing, fellowship and the idea of a collective enterprise. A community of dreamers shares the belief that dreams are valuable. When the community values safety and trust among members and believes that the dreamer knows what his dreams means for himself, communion happens. At its best, dream community is one of the most powerful and intimate forms of community.

Dreams are a powerful catalyst for connection with others. Mention dreams to a group of people, and someone will have a dream to tell. Yet we don't live in a society where sharing dreams is the common practice, so we have to search for people who want to form a dream community.

Guidelines

You can create any kind of dream community you want. It can be leaderless, have rotating leaders or be led by a therapist or dream teacher. It can meet as often as you like. It can include art or drama, or just be a dream-sharing circle.

Because dreams are so intimate, revealing them makes us feel vulnerable. Each dream group needs to agree on a few basic guidelines.

Confidentiality
To establish trust so that good dreamwork can emerge, the group must maintain confidentiality with one another. Members agree that what is revealed stays in the dream circle.

Respect the Mystery and One Another
Avoid interpreting each other's dreams. It is tempting to jump in with an interpretation. Exploring someone else's dream is much easier than deciphering your own, but this undermines the other person's process of becoming a conscious dreamer. Much of the power of group dreamwork lies in the mystery of the dream and the possibilities within it. Mystery needs respect.

When you offer your insights in a thoughtful way, the dreamer can hear herself respond. She can accept or reject the interpretation. Think of dreamwork as the exploration of a new uncharted land. Hold the dream lightly; allow for its ambiguity. Preface your interpretations with phrases like, "To me, this means . . ." or "that

7. CONNECTING WITH OTHER CONSCIOUS DREAMERS

image makes me think of . . . ." Use qualifiers like "may" or "might." These phrases put space around the interpretation. Consider that when a dreamer brings a personal dream to the group, it can have universal meaning.

We benefit from one another's dreams, but the dreamer is the only one who can say what the dream truly means to her. No one has the master key to the meaning of another's dream. Whatever insights you may have about someone else's dream should be offered in a way that helps the dreamer discover the meaning of the dream for herself. Most importantly, the group's insights should not deplete the energy of the dream or undermine the dreamer's unconscious process. Sharing must leave room for the dreamer to discover her own truth—to have a moment of revelation that might make her exclaim "aha!"

It is also very important to allow for the unfolding of each layer of meaning in a dream and not try to tie it up in one interpretation. There is a story about a rabbi named Binza who consulted 24 interpreters about a particular dream. They each gave him a different interpretation, and each interpretation was realized over time.

Learning the Art of Listening

The tone and quality of a dream group is affected by how we listen to each other's dream. Most people don't pay attention to the process of listening. But we can each improve our listening skills.

Listening without interpreting opens up one's capacity to hear more. The best listeners are often the quietest. They remember everyone's imagery and can make associations from long ago dreams. It helps to listen with all of your senses. Even though you may not actively use touch and scent, simply saying, "I want to hear with all of me" will make you more aware of the sensory experience of the dream.

Try listening with your eyes closed. Robert Bosnak, a Jungian analyst and author of *A Little Course on Dreams*, listens this way. He stays open to not knowing what a dream means for as long as possible, while both he and the client hover in a state between waking and sleeping. They work slowly and patiently through a dream. Before a client tells him a dream, he notes all the sensations he is feeling in his body. Then he listens while the dreamer tells the dream and notices any changes in sensations. These become possible entry points for the dreamwork to follow. Very often they lead to surprising, deep inner connections for the dreamer.

Sharing Images as a Couple

Maria felt strongly connected with an image from her boyfriend's dream. She began to work with it, and soon the image became a powerful symbol for her own inner work.

"To me, sharing dreams is an intimacy. First of all, the inner self is exposing itself to me in the dream, which is my being intimate with myself. Then when I share my dream, I expose my inner self to the other. That brings us closer. It generates so much love and fulfillment between us. One morning my boyfriend woke up and told me this dream.

'I dreamed *we were in a river, and there was this shark in the water.*

7. CONNECTING WITH OTHER CONSCIOUS DREAMERS

The shark was covered in jewels. I was scared of it, but you weren't. We both came up out of the water, and then I wasn't as scared of it as when I was in the water.'

Maria told him what it meant to her. "The shark is the lower self or the dark side of us that we are afraid of. The jewels mean that the dark side is really beautiful. The river means the river of life."

When Maria went to her Pathwork session that week, she talked about how powerful this image was for her. "I have created a mask of perfection to hide my cruelty. When I told my Pathwork helper about this dream, she suggested I go to the river and talk to the shark. So I did. In the conversation the shark said, 'I'm very powerful, but I love you.'"

Maria says, "I felt very close to the shark and put my arms around it. It felt like a dolphin, but it was still a shark. We went for a swim. I felt protected because the shark is king of the ocean, and no one would bother us.

"I'm afraid of my hurtful lower self that can rage and attack. But that negative image transformed for me when I swam with the shark. I saw how it can be very connected to the Divine. In the dream the shark symbol of my lower self became a guide, an explorer, and a protector. I continued to dialogue and journey with the shark. The shark is my friend. I actually love the shark. I also looked at the jewels in relation to myself. Could they be a mask I create to cover up the shark in myself? This is a dream that I will work with for a long time. I'm grateful that my boyfriend and I can share imagery in this way."

Group Exercises

1. Wheel of Association

> Every symbol is calculated to rouse us, to wake us up. It is organically tied to energy systems deep in the substrata of the unconscious. When you make a connection that is very close to the energy source, sparks fly.
>
> —Robert A. Johnson

The Wheel of Association exercise works well with a beginning group of dreamers. It is also an easy exercise to do on your own. The dreamer freely associates around key images. This spontaneous opening up to the unconscious gives even the most inexperienced dreamer a wider context for the dream. It also creates a visual representation of the dreamer's language. This exercise is based on John Bradshaw's work in *Healing the Shame that Binds You* [or Robert Johnson's *Inner Work* for a more detailed description.]

Pay attention to where the energy of the dream crests and falls. Think of the valleys and peaks in an electrocardiogram. Listen openly to the dream and select two or three key images to work with. One clue to selecting these images is to look at the symbols you are most strongly attracted to and those you are most repelled by.

I used the Wheel of Association to interpret a dream I had which began with a cryptic remark: *I recognize these energy sweeps. My room is a mess. I have many doll projects to be completed in two days. I know they won't get finished. I have so many doll expressions to paint, as well*

7. CONNECTING WITH OTHER CONSCIOUS DREAMERS

as create their settings. I love them and think I am setting them up for other people like my husband to enjoy, but really they are for me. But they are always incomplete, always needing more work. Why do I have so many projects? Why not one, big, single collection?

I know this dream is like my life—so many interests and difficulty finishing things. But I want to know more about this dream, so I select two images to associate with: (1) many doll projects and (2) one, big, single collection. I make a Wheel of Association for each image.

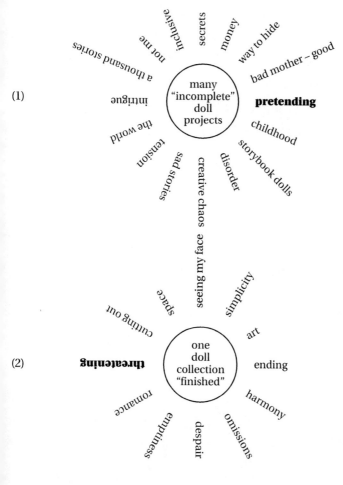

Writing down my associations, I realize I want to put the word *incomplete* in the Many Doll Project circle and the word *finished* in the Single Doll Collection circle. This is the major difference between the two circles.

I scan my associations. As I do this, one word jumps out on each circle: *pretending* for the Many Doll Project and *threatening* for the Single Doll collection. I also have strong feelings about the phrase in the second wheel, *seeing my face*. The dream's meaning moves closer to awareness. I know this because I am feeling nervous about what is being revealed. Even though finishing a single collection would bring harmony and simplicity to my life, it evokes emptiness, despair, and the threat of seeing something I've been resisting knowing. This is probably why I surround myself with unfinished projects.

I go deeper. I make a wheel of association with *dolls*.

This time, two associations feel very strong: *Demeter* and *escape*. I realize they represent the split in my mother between her desire to mother and her desire to *escape*. I wonder how much of my unfinished creativity has to do with this unconscious dilemma.

John Bradshaw tells us these "split parts of ourselves are full of energy." By listening to the energy of the dream, we discover the parts of ourselves that we have disowned or lost from consciousness. In this exercise, one person guides the dreamer through the process of making associations. The rest of the group witnesses their exchange, noting their own responses to it. When the dreamer is finished, make time for group sharing. Any dream worked on in a group will touch other people's inner worlds. Remember to refrain from interpreting the dream. Also be aware that the dreamer has just been involved in a deep process and needs time to assimilate the imagery and practice the ritual.

Steps For Exploring the Wheel of Association In a Group Setting

- The dreamer chooses someone from the group to be the helper for her work. This person will be the record keeper of the imagery and associations and will encourage the dreamer whenever she gets stuck. The helper keeps the work moving if the dreamer is tempted to stop the process when revealing material emerges.
- The helper asks the dreamer to tell the dream twice. In the first telling you pay attention to the energy; in the second, you listen for details and images.
- As you listen to the first reading, pay attention to how the dreamer is telling the dream. Your feeling responses are valuable to this

process. Note where you feel an increase of energy, either positive or negative, in the telling of the dream. Also note what part(s) of the dream attract or repel you.
- Pay attention to your response and to the dreamer's energy. Notice where you feel most engaged and where you feel no energy. Has your interest peaked, while the dreamer shows little affect? If so, this may be an area of resistance in the dreamer.
- After the first reading, the helper makes a list of key images, such as a person, object, situation, color, sound, or phrase.
- Then the dreamer retells the dream and selects an image or two. It may be a potent image or even one of the least likely ones. On a sheet of plain paper, the helper draws a circle large enough to contain the name of one image. Leave plenty of space outside the circle for the dreamer's associations.
- Concentrating on one image at a time, the dreamer speaks whatever comes to mind: feelings, other images, words, or ideas. He lets the associations come spontaneously. When the dreamer comes to a natural stop, the helper asks if there are more associations.
- When the dreamer is finished, the helper reads all of the associations, asking the dreamer which one he resonates with most.
- The dreamer explores how these associations and images relate to his inner and outer life—to the emotions and blind spots, to his relationships and problem areas.
- From the associations, the dreamer makes an interpretative statement about the dream's meaning.
- Then it is time to create a ritual or practice that will carry this dream into the dreamer's waking life. [Chapter three]

7. CONNECTING WITH OTHER CONSCIOUS DREAMERS

- The rest of the dream group then shares their own associations and connections to the dream and its images.

Solo Wheel

When doing this exercise alone, you follow the steps above, but without a helper. You must pay attention to your own responses because they are the route to your unconscious. Listen with all of your senses. Reread your dream, perhaps aloud.

- Notice which feelings arise as you reread the dream: tension, excitement, boredom, fear, joy, other?
- At what points in the dream are you experiencing specific sensations?
- Select the image you have the most feelings about, and/or the one you have the least feelings for.
- Make your Wheel of Association and continue as you would if you were in a group process.

2. "If it Were my Dream..."

This exercise is a simple but powerful way of relating to another person's dream as if it were your own. [Two leaders in the field of dreamwork, Montague Ullman and Jeremy Taylor, created it independently from each other.] In this dream process group members enter together into a single dream. As a listener, you project yourself into the dream as if it were your own. In the process you receive a personal message from the dream and offer a possible new meaning to the dreamer. This process enriches everyone.

One day Ingrid brought a simple dream to one of my groups. It had a metaphorical and archetypal quality to it that would lend itself well to this exercise. So Ingrid told us her dream:

"I meet a man with two grown-up sons and I feel very attracted to both sons. They are foreigners who don't speak the language well. They are dark, maybe Gypsies. One son asks me to marry him, and although I would have rather married the other one, I say yes because they are brothers and they are similar. What I really want is to be part of that family. We all live together in a big apartment house. On the first night of our marriage, my husband does not come home and I am enraged. I go to his father and tell him that if my husband is not home by 6:00 the next night, I will have the marriage annulled. Then I am shown a picture to tell me why my husband is not here. The picture shows my husband carrying his old violin teacher, who is very sick and fragile. He is taking him to a hospital. Knowing that reconciles me, and I feel I made the right choice in marrying this man because the other brother would certainly not have done this."

She repeats the dream, so we can fill our awareness with it. When she finishes, we sit quietly with it, imagining it to be our own dream. One by one we retell it as a dream that is ours, beginning with "If it were my dream . . . ." We let ourselves enter the dream, and speak from the place where the dream is happening in us now. There is quiet between each of the retellings. As we go around the circle, the new dream we are weaving gathers more power and begins to reveal its many layers. We are letting the dream reflect our individual personalities. For one, the dream speaks of a choice of faith or blindness. For others it is about such issues as acceptance of

7. CONNECTING WITH OTHER CONSCIOUS DREAMERS

one's destiny; distrust of father; appreciation; and personal relationship with God and his two golden sons, Jesus and Lucifer.

There is silence when we have finished, the silence of awe. Ingrid tells us how valuable this was for her. She describes the part of each of our stories that she resonates with. She compares this experience to the first time she went through this process, when she felt her dream was being taken away from her. She realizes how much she trusts us to be a part of her life. Today we do not take from her dream; we deepen it.

Steps for "If it were my dream . . ."

A short, cohesive dream works best for this process since a long, meandering one is harder for the listeners to remember.

- The dreamer tells the dream twice.
- The listeners ask questions about the dream in order to sharpen their ability to see, sense, and experience it for themselves. This is the time to clarify details so that you can enter the dream fully.
- Allow for quiet time before you begin. This will enable each dreamer to focus, enter the dream, and let it become hers.
- One by one, each person in the circle tells the story of her dream, beginning with "If it were my dream . . ." Sometimes I begin with the phrase "In my dream . . ."

There are no right or wrong ways to organize your dream story. You may include your associations to the dream or offer your own ending. Trust that when you enter the dream what you reveal may be helpful to the dreamer, as well as to you.

- Allow for pauses between each person's dream story so the dreamer can absorb it and register any recognition.
- When everyone has contributed, the original dreamer shares what she resonated with in the dream stories.
- A variation on this process has each person drawing a picture of the dream and then sharing the picture and story.

3. Group Dramatization

Dramatizing a dream is a powerful group experience.

- One dreamer offers a dream and becomes its director.
- Before the dream is brought to life, the dreamer asks a question of the dream and indicates which character or symbol in the dream has the answer.
- The dreamer tells the dream twice, while everyone listens.
- Then the dreamer selects a person for each character and symbol in the dream, including inanimate and animal figures.
- The chosen actors ask questions, focusing on the five senses and the emotions, in order to ground the dream in their own experience. They do not ask analytic or interpretive questions.
- The actors imagine the dream for themselves and pay attention to the emotional quality of the dream.
- Once all the questions have been asked, the dreamer becomes the audience while the rest of the group re-enacts the dream.
- As the dream unfolds, the characters can continue the dream, allowing their collective, intuitive vision to guide them to its completion.

Having your dream enacted before your eyes can be transformational for you. Maria had such an experience:

7. CONNECTING WITH OTHER CONSCIOUS DREAMERS

"The time our group enacted a dream for me was the first time I was able to really clearly see the message in my dreams. Prior to that I dealt with the surface of my dreams. When I dreamed about someone else, I'd think maybe I should give this person a call or the dream was about him or her. But this time I realized it was all about me. It was a message from my soul.

I am going to school in Connecticut, and I don't know why I am there. I am with a counselor who is going to guide me through orientation. He is tall with blue eyes, a very relaxed person. I keep saying, 'I don't know why I am here. I have all these degrees.' I show him my resume with all my degrees and credentials and where I had worked. He says not to worry. But I am very concerned that I don't need to be there. Also in the dream is a cousin I haven't seen for a while who has sent me a picture of the place where I am going to be living. Suddenly I am transported to that place. I look out of the window and there are horses grazing. They are just 'being' there. Just grazing and swatting with their tails.

"The feeling I had in the dream was anxiety. It didn't have any meaning to me. It was just images. Before we enacted the dream, I remember Raechel said that maybe Connecticut was important. Why Connecticut? Someone pointed out the word *connect*. Raechel said, 'Maybe you're needing connection.' I felt some recognition, but as I watched this dream being acted out, the light bulb went on.

"I realized that the school I was going to in the dream had to do with connecting to *being*, not *doing*. Although it's a very simple message, it had a lot of impact for me. I was overactive at the time, working in a busy city hospital, and my soul was longing to be like the horses in the field. I had been hoping that being so productive was going to fulfill me. It never does. It only does when you have the serenity to go with it.

"The people acting as the horses were slow-moving and relaxed. Watching them, I knew immediately what it meant. I hadn't expected them to be this way. The dream had been fuzzy, but watching it played out, it all clicked. Everything in the dream was relaxed but me. The horses were relaxed. The counselor was relaxed. The feeling I was getting from them was very rich, rich in the *being*, in the calmness and serenity. The counselor was like a guide, a guiding counselor. I had many things on my resume to show all that I was *doing*, but the quality in me was anxiety. It is not important what is on my resume. What matters is my being calm and more receptive.

"The longing to be, and graze, and sit in the sun has stayed with me. I give that to myself now. Even when I am *doing*, I feel more balanced. I'm doing yoga. I have a meditative practice. My activity has a better quality to it. The quality of my midwifery has changed. Now I am in a practice that focuses on one woman at a time so I can be more relaxed in my *doing*."

The Evolution of a Dream Community

A group that meets regularly over time, especially one that uses a variety of techniques, may find its dreams evolving. One such group met with me for several years, then continued on their own at each other's homes. Over time, as members came to trust one another more deeply and became more familiar with each other's imagery, the group took on its present form. They began to dream for one

7. CONNECTING WITH OTHER CONSCIOUS DREAMERS

another. They found themselves weaving in and out of each other's dreams. They recognized the content of their daily lives as dream symbols, as well. They are a true dream community, holding one another's lives sacred.

In their current evolution they have become such an invaluable source of support and wisdom for one another that they have made a commitment to keep the group going until death. They are now in their 11th year of semi-monthly meetings.

A Conscious Dreamer: John

John is a professional artist whose dreams are close to his awareness. He gives himself a lot of time for contemplation. He mulls over his dreams and shares them with his wife. While his work as an artist is done alone, he knows he needs community to help him unravel his dreams.

When John had this dream, he was in one of my dream communities. He had a major painting show coming up the following month and was feeling a lot of fear. As he said, "Mostly self-search was going on. I was looking in on anger. Before this, I was polite towards anger, but separate. I did not acknowledge the amount of anger in me. I would have said anger was not a driving force in me.

"I brought a dream I had titled *Shut into a Huge Cage at a Zoo* to the dream group.

"*The dream starts in a large cage, 60 to 70 square meters with huge bars. It is up against the outside wall of a building. A filthy cage. The floor is covered with straw and mountains of black shit. There's an elephant, a gorilla, an invisible black bear and me. You can feel the presence of this black bear, but he can't be seen. There is also an invisible woman in the cage. I am invisible in this cage, too. I am the invisible man, watching things. The woman and I cling to the bars on the sides of the cage. We don't go down so we won't step in the shit on the bottom. In the middle of the cage is a smaller house with a roof.*

"*At some point in the dream, the elephant gets into a real fury, thrashing about. The black bear and the gorilla and I are hanging from the bars, trying to stay out of the way, trying to escape. We are afraid of the*

7. CONNECTING WITH OTHER CONSCIOUS DREAMERS

anger of this elephant. He is stuck down there in the shit, angry. We are afraid, yet we know we, too, are this anger. We all converge on the roof and cower while the elephant thrashes about, mad with anger. Suddenly the woman and I are on the outside of the cage, looking down, talking about what is happening. Now I have a body, and I am wearing a suit. We are in an observation booth talking to each other about getting back into the cage. There is no way in. The bars will stop us. We can't pass through the bars. There's a photocopy machine beside us. So we pass ourselves over the photocopy machine, and as pieces of paper we can slide between the bars and get back inside the cage. Once inside we are clinging to the bars again. The elephant is still thrashing about, menacing us. He strikes out at the woman and rips her dress, top to bottom. She recovers herself as best as possible. There is nothing outside of the cage except white light. No world outside the cage."

The group decided to enact the dream. As the director, John selected people to play the different characters. Then he watched as they brought the dream to life, projecting their perceptions into the characters and allowing the dream to evolve.

"I was absolutely amazed at the clarity, how others picked up right away the elephant being part of me. Before that, I took the dream too literally. The invisible woman was probably my animus, suppressed. On my own, I would get a dream like this and see just an invisible woman. My initial interpretations protect myself. When the group acted the dream out, I couldn't hide or deny the real story that was being told in the dream.

"It was me in the cage with other parts of my personality. I was trapped in some cage, and there was a lot of shit. The part of me stuck in the shit was the elephant. The other parts of me could get away, but the elephant is furious and is threatening my other parts. My unintentional protection is to watch myself from an observation booth.

"I can admit the truth to myself up to a certain point. After that, I have to be guided. I rarely volunteer to go myself. I always need help to play with my dreams. I need to be pushed further in order to go deeper into the dream. And so, with help, I was able to re-enter the dream and make subtle changes; I went from being a frightened victim to a participant."

John knew theoretically that he had a lot of anger to deal with. He could articulate the painful details of his childhood, but he kept his uncomfortable feelings at a distance. After working with this dream, he knew anger in his gut, not just in his head.

"I classify my dreams in two ways. One being amusing, frightening, or fantasy dreams, the other being educational dreams. These last dreams have such a strong feeling that whatever went on in the dream is of great significance to me. These are the dreams I ask questions of.

"The elephant dream is one of those. The dream is asking me many questions. What would have happened if the dream continued? Did the elephant get over his anger? Why was the invisible woman invisible? What was gorilla? Is it the side of me that is capable of menacing, that threatening part which just by virtue of existence creates fear? Is the elephant the wise animal, but has no alternative but to stand in the shit? Is my wisdom stuck in the shit? Where have we gone (all these aspects of John)? What

7. CONNECTING WITH OTHER CONSCIOUS DREAMERS

happened to elephant in my life? What happened in my day-to-day life to invisible woman and to gorilla? In my maleness I want a resolution. A fairy tale. They all lived happily ever after."

John is stuck with these questions, and with a feeling of incompleteness and "convoluted imagery," at the end of the group. His personal commitment is to continue growing spiritually, and so, over time, he will discover the relevant answers. As he says, "The answer is *Stay tuned*. We'll find out.'"

PART THREE:

Staying Awake

The Imaginal Journey

The Seeds

The seeds begin abstract as their species,
remote as the name on the sack
they are carried home in: Fayette Seed Company
Corner of Vine and Rose. But the sower
going forth to sow sets foot
into time to come, the seeds falling
on his own place. He has prepared a way
for his life to come to him, if it will.
Like a tree, he has given roots
to the earth, and stands free.

—Wendell Berry

Personal imagery comes in dreams, but it can also be accessed through the waking visualization known as the imaginal journey. These voyages of the imagination are like Wendell Berry's seeds. They allow us to step into "time to come" and to prepare a way for life to come to us. They show us possibilities we might not see otherwise. They reveal how we are living, how to plant seedlings, and how to let them root.

My personal dreamwork has always been enriched by imaginal journeys. They nourish and inform my nightly dreams. Both the dream and the waking journey link the conscious self with the soul. Although the focus of this book has been on nighttime dreams and the ways of working with them consciously, I wanted to include several imaginal journeys to encourage and develop your sensing and intuitive capacities. They will improve your receptivity to dreams.

When you enter waking imaginal space, you work with the symbolic language of your dreams. Using your five senses heightens the experience of waking dream reality. Each journey begins with an induction to lead you into the realm of your imagination, and follows with an open-ended journey that evokes the dreamlike experience. The induction helps you relax, let go of your distractions, and move your attention to an inner place. The framework orients you within your imagination. Its spaciousness allows your own personal imagery to arise into your awareness.

The imaginal journeys in this chapter were inspired by the teachings of Madame Colette Muscat of Jerusalem, and by teachers of her work: Dr. Judith Schmidt and Dr. Francis Clifton.

How to do an Imaginal Journey

To do an imaginal journey by yourself, first tape record the induction and journey. Read the induction in a quiet voice, and then use a direct style and more vibrant tone of voice for the journey. The quieter voice will help you drop into the imaginal space without going to sleep. A more vibrant tone will help you stay alert on the journey. When you play back the tape, use the pause button to allow time for your imagery to emerge and evolve. If you are doing a journey with a partner or in a group, one person can guide the other.

If you are surprised by the images that appear, this is good; it means your mind is not controlling what you see. If you want to reject what appears, trust the spontaneity of the image and don't discard it too quickly.

You may find you want to go in a different direction than the journey suggests. Do so rather than getting involved in a mental struggle. Trust that your greater self knows what you need and where to lead you. Don't worry if you go to a different place. If you do these journeys more than once, you will find that each experience is different.

The induction takes you into your imagination through a golden circle. The journey guides you once you are there. At the end of the journey, return your awareness to the room, back through the golden circle. Take time to orient yourself. Become aware of the chair you are sitting on, the floor beneath your feet, and other sensations of being in the waking world.

When you are ready, draw and write your imagery. Then create your own spiritual practice.

Inductions to Use With Any Imaginal Journey

Some people prefer a quick induction and rapid journey. Others like to enter dream space slowly. I have included inductions of both styles. The short version comes from Dr. Francis Clifton, the longer one from Dr. Judith Schmidt.

Choose one of these two inductions to use before any of the journeys in this chapter.

Sit in a place where you will be comfortable. It is preferable to sit rather than to lie down, which can induce sleep. You want to be relaxed but alert.

1. Short Form Induction

Close your eyes. Let yourself come to your breathing naturally. Be aware of any places that are tight in you. Gently send your breath there to relax the tightness.

Breathe in through your nose and exhale long and slowly through your mouth. See yourself breathing in blue golden light and breathing out gray smoke.

Breathe in the blue gold of the sun. Let this blue golden light relax your body.

Breathe out a gray, stale smoke, releasing all that is old and used up in you.

Breathe in all that is pure.

Breathe out all that is impure.

Breathe in all that is nourishing.

Breathe out all that is waste.

As you form this even and regular pattern of breathing, know that you are turning your senses inward to the center of yourself, the realm of your imagination.

Now with each exhalation, begin to count backwards from three to two to one. When you reach one, know that you have reached your Oneness.

Breathe out to zero. See before you a golden circle large enough for you to stand in. Stand in the golden circle. Step through the circle and . . . [begin the journey here.]

2. Long Form Induction

Close your eyes. Bring your awareness to your breath—your natural way of breathing. Be aware of your breath entering your nostrils . . . and leaving your nostrils . . . your breath rising and falling . . . Do not make your breath do anything . . . Continue to breathe in this way, quietly aware of breathing in . . . breathing out . . . Just sensing the breath entering through your nose—the mystery of that—how it never stops.

Be aware of any tension you may be holding in your body: any discomfort or stress, emotional or physical. Allow your awareness to move slowly through your body. When you come to a tight or held place, either physical or emotional, breathe into that place. Gently release the tension . . . Relax your body.

Return your awareness to your breathing in . . . breathing out . . . breathing in new breath . . . exhaling old breath . . . breathing in . . . breathing out.

Now begin to see a color or colors being drawn in by your

breath . . . See a healing color . . . Carry this color along your breath to a place inside you that needs healing . . . Breathe this color into the part of your body that needs healing. Continue breathing in . . . breathing out.

See this healing light moving through your veins, filling your body with its radiant color . . . Continue to breathe this color throughout your body as your breath rises and falls . . . until your entire body, out to the very edges of your skin, is filled with this healing light.

Be aware of how your breath breathes you . . . of its precious mystery . . . this breath . . . this healing light.

Now see this healing light surrounding your entire body . . . from the top of your head to the bottom of your feet . . . in back and in front of you . . . until you are filled inside and outside with this light.

Now with each exhalation, count backward from three . . . to two . . . to one. Know that you have come to the source of your imagination . . . to the place of your Oneness . . . where you are all you can be and all that you are.

Breathe back to zero. Let the zero become a golden circle . . . large enough for you to stand in . . . Step into the golden circle . . .

Now step through the golden circle, and . . . [go into the journey you have selected]

Imaginal Journey of the Seven Sleepers

The story of the Seven Sleepers is a key to understanding dreamwork and also a wonderful way to enter the dream cave. Here is the dreamlike way I enter this legend and imagine the experiences of the Seven Sleepers.

This journey focuses on the individual within the collective. Whenever you need to restore your spirit, you will find this an invaluable journey. Through it you will receive your inner wisdom and the wisdom of the collective. Use this journey for healing the self, for healing the collective and for receiving answers to your personal questions.

Though this is a long journey, it has natural breaks. You can do it all at once, or you may wish to do one section of the journey each week for a seven-week period. If you are doing the latter, remember to use the induction with each weekly journey.

When you have completed all seven sections, your weekly reflections will reveal which parts were most powerful and which ones to repeat. They will also show how the journey has entered and affected you.

Journey
Follow the induction, then . . .

I. See, sense, and experience yourself in a place that is special to you. It may be a place you know. It may be a place you imagine. Just let the image of this place arise spontaneously. Look around and see what this haven looks like. Listen to the sounds in this place. Sense the air. If there is something to taste in this place, taste it. Feel the ground beneath your feet.

Here in your haven, become aware of a situation in your life that is troubling you. See yourself sitting with this difficult situation, holding it in your awareness.

See and sense who comes to you. Tell this being about the difficulty you are having. See this being giving you what you need to heal this problem. Receive this gift. Trust that your imagination and your heart will bring you what you need. Thank this being.

Breathe out . . .

II. See, sense, and experience yourself going into the land of your troubles, perhaps in the presence of those in disagreement with you, or those who will be affected by your resolution of this problem. See yourself carrying the gifts you received in your special haven. Experience yourself standing true to yourself.

Breathe out . . .

III. See, sense, and experience yourself choosing to go apart from the conflict. See yourself packing a small pack. See what you take with you. Hear yourself saying good-bye to those around you. See who they are. Experience your parting.

Sense yourself traveling away from your haven . . . into the mountains. See the path you walk and the way it leads you up the mountainside. Feel the air and all that you sense along this path. See yourself coming to a cave. Sense your feelings as you explore the entrance. See and know who comes to join you as you enter the cave. Experience walking into the cave, coming to your ritual space. See how you gather in a circle. Sense this circle. Know what you give to others in this cave. See and sense what you receive from them.

    Breathe out . . .

IV. See, sense, and experience yourself lying down with your companions in the cave to sleep and dream. Know what needs healing in your life. Dream a healing dream. See and experience this dream. Take all the time you need to complete your dream.

    Breathe out . . .

V. See and know the dreams of the other dreamers in the cave with you. Experience the healing of their dreams. Know how your dream gives to them. Know what you receive from their dreams.

    Breathe out . . .

VI. See and know the collective dream, dreamed by all of you in the cave. See and sense your collective dream rising into the air and going out into all the land. See where it goes. See and experience it bringing healing to the world.

    Breathe out . . .

VII. See, sense, and experience yourself awakening from the dream. Take all the time you need to see each of the people in your dream cave. See them awaken. Experience your reunion into waking. See and sense what you do as you emerge from the cave. See what you have awakened to: what wonders your dreams have wrought in the land of your troubles.

See, sense, and experience yourself returning to your home. Know that you carry within you the powerful changes of the dreaming you have done in this dream cave. See these changes manifesting. Know how you have given to this transformation.

Breathe out . . .

Slowly return back through the golden circle into the room. Feel your feet on the floor. Sense the chair beneath you. Gently open your eyes. Take time to write or draw what you experienced.

Journeys for Special Purposes

Incubating a Dream

Follow the induction, then . . .

See, sense, and experience yourself coming to an incubation cave. See where the cave is. Know that you have come here to receive the highest dream wisdom. Near the entrance you find a waterfall and pool. See and sense yourself bathing in this pool. Sense the washing away of your cares. Leave the pool and find beside it a new set of clothing. See what it looks like. Put it on. Know what needs healing and why you have come to this cave for a dream.

See yourself entering the cave. Sense the atmosphere and feel the temperature. If possible, see the walls, floor and ceiling. See the furnishings in this cave. See who tends the cave. See how you prepare to lie down and receive your dream. Know what you ask of the dream.

See yourself sleeping, and dreaming a healing dream . . . or receiving the deeper truth of the dream you have brought into this cave.

When you awaken from your dream, return to the waking world. Feel the chair beneath you. Feel the floor beneath your feet. Take time to write or draw what you experienced.

Connecting with Your Soul's Desire

> When the soul wishes to experience something, she throws an image of the experience out before her and enters into her own image.
>
> —Meister Eckhart

Follow the induction, then . . .

See, sense, and experience yourself standing on flat land. See the sun behind you and your shadow in front of you. Feel the air on your skin. See and sense your surroundings.

Sense your soul standing behind you and throwing out before you an image that your soul wishes you to know and to experience. When you see this image before you, send your shadow out to surround it. Draw a line around the outline of the image and your shadow.

See yourself going to join your shadow around your soul's desire. Sense your soul's support and blessings for living out this desire.

Know that when you and your shadow have joined, you are successful and whole, having entered into your soul's new way of being. Sense yourself living out this new image. Take all the time you need to sense yourself entering into this new vision. See yourself going forth into this new way of being. When you are ready, return to the room. Sense the chair and floor beneath you. Hear the sounds around you. Write or draw your newfound image or understanding.

Slumbering Seeds

> Happiness and love follow truth—the commitment to truth, whatever it may be. Deep in your heart is the seed for all these potentials: truth, love, happiness, wisdom, and peace. You possess these attributes, these states of being, in ample quantity and quality. It is up to you to realize them, which you do by first conceiving of these potentialities deep inside of your innermost being. You then conceive of spreading out these slumbering potentials, to awaken and spread them outward, so that they grow from within into the outer regions of your life.
>
> —Eva Pierrakos
> *The Evolutionary Process*

Follow the induction, then . . .

See yourself in a garden with empty planting beds. See what the sky looks like. See what time of day it is. See the seeds of your heart. See where they are and know how they slumber, waiting to be planted. See what these seeds hold. See yourself planting them. Know in what way you need to tend them so they will grow. Take all the time you need in your garden to plant and care for these seeds.

Suggested practice: Go to the garden each day and tend the seeds. See what unfolds.

Journey for a Dream Community

Follow the induction, then . . .

See, sense, and experience yourself approaching a temple. See where this temple is situated. Sense your surroundings. Feel the air. See the time of day or night. Experience yourself entering this temple. Be aware of the light inside the temple.

In this sacred space you find a group of urns. Know that each urn belongs to one of the people in your dream circle. Sense yourself walking around and looking at each of these urns. See how they differ from one another. Look at their individual shapes and patterns.

Find your own urn in the temple. Be with your urn. Know what it holds. Sense what it is like to be with your urn.

Know that at the dark time of year in this temple, there is a celebration of the light. Sense the preparations being made for this celebration soon to come. Your part is to polish the urns. In the temple you have all you need for polishing them.

See yourself going to each urn. Know what part of each urn needs polishing. Experience yourself polishing each one. See what happens. Take all the time you need to polish these urns and make them shine. Experience the feelings of giving to these holy preparations, knowing you will partake in this celebration with those you care about. When you are ready to leave the temple, return to the room. Sense the chair and floor beneath you. Find a way to creatively express what you discovered.

Dreams of Awe

> ... Perhaps while dreaming, the hand that
> sowed the seed of stars
> struck a chord of old forgotten music
>
> and like a note from a great harp
> the faint wave arrives at our lips
> in just a few honest words.
>
> —Antonio Machado
> *Translated by David Whyte*

Dreams can be broadly sorted into four categories. *Dream baths* wash away the grime of the day. These usually do not require our close attention. *Prescient dreams* foretell the future and are confirmed by matching them with events in waking reality. Most dreams are *workhorse dreams*, which confront us with calls to change or give us a mirror to look at our lives. These are the repetitive messages the soul sends in their many variations until we respond to them. But there is a dream that the conscious dreamer treasures above all the others—*the dream of awe*. This is the rarest of dreams; we may have only a few our lifetime. These dreams have a depth and profound knowing that sustain us and invite us to the mountaintop.

In *The Way of Woman* Helen M. Luke describes the significance of this kind of imagery. "When images of power and beauty rise up in dreams or fantasies, they make an immediate impact. We are in awe before them. Sometimes there comes a specific dream of initiation, which may alter the whole course of a man's life. Such images are not something thought up or pried into, they cannot be altered, and instinctively we sense that they must not be spoken of except to another 'initiate.' When one does expose them wrongly, one can feel the power go out of them."

Dreams of awe can uplift and carry us through difficult places. They can be shocking, making us look at our darkest depths. They can be mysterious, arising from the mists, only to be spoken of to other "initiates" of the mystery. They encourage us to work with the hard places in our lives. They help us face what is most difficult to see. They remind us there is light after darkness.

Dreams of awe always appear unexpectedly. We cannot control when or how we will receive them. We can only give ourselves the spaciousness these dreams need to bless us; in return we honor them with our remembering.

The dreams that follow are being shared with you, as one dreamer to another, in respect for the willingness of all of us to go on this sacred journey of awakening and evolving consciousness.

I received a dream of awe while vacationing alone in a tiny village in Languedoc, France, several years ago. Prior to having the dream, I had spent several days walking, painting, and writing, so I was an open channel to spirit. One night I asked for a dream that would guide me in writing a book about working with dreams. I was awakened at 1:00 A.M., realizing that I had received a holy healing dream.

I am working in a clinic, where a thirteen year-old girl with hip and back ailments is awaiting surgery. The doctor says it is best to do it while she is a child. I say to him, "Not when you are thirteen. Then you are filled with all sorts of strong emotions. This is a much more intense time and she won't forget." I tell the child she can call on me for anything. Then I leave her and find myself standing near the healer in charge of the clinic. I am leaking energy out the back of my pelvis. I know the healer is weary from the day, so I tell him I only want to sit at his feet and absorb his energy. I stay near him, not speaking. He moves behind me, places his pelvis against my lower back and begins to pour Christ's energy through himself into me, filling the wound with the sweetest, most powerful light. I waken from the dream and lie still for a long time, continuing to be bathed in this exquisite energy.

In the morning I recorded the rest of the night's dreams, which seemed banal compared to this holiest of dreams. I was amazed that the ordinary and extraordinary could live so easily side-by-side. I spent the next days painting, writing, and meditating on this dream, realizing that I had been afraid of allowing my healing current to flow with my heart because it was confused with my wounded, sexual current. I knew I had been in the presence of the Great Healer; I felt like Mary Magdalene and the woman who touched Jesus' hem and was healed. When I returned home, I discovered that Languedoc is believed to have been the home of Mary Magdalene after Jesus' death, and that people living there today still revere her.

I carried this dream in my heart for years. I believe it was a soul healing, as well as a vision for my life as a healer. It was also a foreshadowing of a long-term healing process. Seven years later, at the culmination of a lengthy therapy and study of Kabbalistic healing, I embarked on an intensive month of physical, emotional and spiritual healing work with an Integrated Kabbalistic Healer. This healer was the Dr. Kim of my octopus dream and an associate of the healer in this dream of awe. Through our work together, the leakage point in my psyche was repaired. The thirteen-year-old in me no longer had to seep out of me in search of love and reflection. At last I could stand my own ground of truth even if it meant discomfort in others or their possible rejection of me.

Frank, Millie, and Michael all relate their own dreams of awe.

Frank is a successful executive in the corporate world. He has achieved his position through his intellect and strong will. In recent years he has been opening the dam to his emotions and has discovered that he is a deeply feeling man. In midlife he is going through many internal changes and upheavals. These can be turbulent.

Frank had two significant dreams of the ocean a year apart. The first dream set the stage for the second dream, which was clearly a dream of awe to him. Both dreams continue to sustain him in stressful times in his personal and professional life.

His first dream may seem ordinary. Yet to Frank it was a powerful experience. His work with this three-sentence dream, which he calls his "supertanker dream," ensured that it would become life-long imagery. A small dream can have profound effects when it is not discarded.

"I am on a boat far out in the ocean with huge rolling waves like mountains. I am scared. Ahead I see the Scotland Light Ship, a ship I have often seen in waking life off the coast near my home."

When Frank re-entered the dream space, he discovered that the iridescent white anchor line went straight into the water. It rose up and down with the ship's movement, but he was not afraid because the ship was obviously anchored. When the next huge rollers came, he could feel the sensation in his body. Frank dialogued with the anchor, which said, "I'm white because I want everyone to see me. At the bottom of my line is a spade anchor, strongly attached to the bottom. I can let my ship swing around to best handle the swells and waves. I am anchored strong and deep."

The Scotland Light Ship was double-ended. As long as the bow or the stern turned into the waves, it was safe. It was always in view. Frank saw a smaller boat, a pilot ship, attached to the Scotland Light Ship, which could carry him back and forth from land to the Scotland Light Ship. When he was on the pilot ship or out on the deck or masts of the Scotland Light Ship, he didn't like the feeling of being out of control. Here he had to block out the rolling with his will. He felt better being inside near the engines. Frank dialogued with the engine, which said, "I'm the ballast when the ship is tied. I'm bolted down to the hull. I'm the part of Frank that he is not aware of. I'm the deeply rootedness of him. I want to remind him that he knows I am here."

Frank accepted the idea that waves are supposed to roll, and that a tanker with an anchor will carry him safely through the roughest waves. The Scotland Light Ship is a beacon for him in stormy times. He uses this dream to anchor him when his outer life, with its deep emotional waves, threatens to overwhelm him.

A year later Frank had a dream of awe. At the time he was sleeping in a tent alone at a campsite. The dream shocked him wide-awake.

"I am at the ocean. Several of my friends and I are surfing. I'm on a stretch of beach on Long Beach Island (New Jersey). There is a huge line of waves rolling in. It's early morning. The sky is clear and the sun is shimmering. The feeling is excitement, mixed with some apprehension. Suddenly I am down in the swells and a huge wave is coming. I am paddling like crazy. I have the physical sensation of going up and up like an elevator. This isn't fun anymore. My buddies are not making it to the top of this 'mother of all waves.' This is a ten-story wave. I am thrown into the curl and my feet are up and I am about to be overwhelmed, when suddenly I am up and over the top. And I see another wave coming. I woke up, gripping my air mattress and shaking."

Reentering the dream later, Frank rode the huge wave to the top and saw an oncoming wave. This time, in the distance, there was a huge mammal swimming towards him from the north. It was part whale and part porpoise. The sky had darkened. Frank was alone.

The wave spoke, "I come from a long way off with enormous amounts of energy. I come from across the ocean, where wind and water and sun come together in a place of creation. I have no consciousness. I am only pure energy. When I break, I break for miles.

I crash. I die. I dissipate my energy. I have no mission. I have no direction. I am constantly moving. Whoever or whatever is in my way, I lift up."

The dolphin/whale spoke, "I am breath. I am life. Nothing gets in my way. I want to see this being who rode over the big wave. If he is out here in the waves, he has to be responsible for himself. Now that he's out this far, he can't go back. After he is out here for a while, it will get smoother." Then the dolphin/whale swam on, going toward the south.

Frank continued to explore this dream imaginally. He came through calm, languid, brighter waters to an island with big stone sculptures on the shore. He rode his surfboard into a quiet inlet where he could see houses on each side—golden ones on one side and silver on the other.

This state of being was new to Frank, who was used to being in charge. He knows how to surf, how to select a wave to ride, when to catch it, and where he must be on the wave at all times. He is not used to riding his board in deep, calm waters.

In his imaginal journey, Frank discovered he could lie on the board, hands at his sides. He felt the sun on his body and smelled the sea. He knew a part of him was alert while a part of him was resting.

As he floated on top of the ocean waters he saw the waters of the Virgin Islands, where he had snorkeled in the past. To one side the ocean floor dropped off dramatically. He was afraid of the dark unknown depths and wondered what might come up from there. He wanted to do something, but there was nothing to do. He did not even know what he needed. All he could do was be on the board.

Since the dream, Frank waits in this space. His emotional life continues to open to deeper feelings. He is amazed when waves of tears pour through him, but he has the truth of these dreams—of his real anchor, inside. He trusts where he is going.

Since he likes to surf, it is a natural image for him; he can relate to it physically and emotionally. This experience helps his awareness of the metaphors of this dream and his life expand. Exploring the dream, he realizes that the waves are opportunities and challenges in his life. He no longer needs the support of his supertanker. He has gained enough inner strength to handle his emotional waves. He can ride life's depths as if he is on a surfboard.

Millie had a dream of awe while vacationing in Provence, France. One day she and her husband visited the Cistercian abbey at Sénanque, the oldest monastery in the world.

"This is a very plain, monastic chapel in the shape of a cross. After our tour, I went to the Vespers service and sat through the chanting. My husband, who stood in the back, made note that I was the only one swaying with the French chant. That night I had a sacred dream.

"*I am at the Cistercian chapel, which now is all brick but very soft with no edges, and the three parts of the cross flow together. Then St. Michael comes in wounded and beaten up, bloodied by the battles and evil forces of our world. He's come into the sanctuary to be healed. Am I to heal him? How can I heal him?*

"*I notice the images of Christ on the left, Buddha on the right, and the magnificent light of God shining in the center. God's energy is flowing into all the parts and healing St. Michael. This is the light of God healing everyone, everything, but particularly St. Michael.*

"I am standing on the first level, in the center, in front of the light. The Christ and the Buddha are on the second level, and God is on the third. The altar is behind me. St. Michael is prostrate in front of the Christ. I go to him and try to comfort him. I am healing him by touching him. He is receptive to me. I am praying to the Creator, 'May he be well because the world needs him so badly.'

"Immediately after the dream I was elated. It was so peaceful and invigorating that I felt a deep sense of peace. Whenever I remember it, I feel comforted. It's become a sanctuary I go to when I am hurting, even though I cannot access the dream's original intensity.

"Once in a guided imaginal journey, I returned to this chapel where I knew the light of God. I found eight special urns. One was broken. But I'm afraid of this dream. It almost seems like I'm being sacrilegious. I was raised Catholic, yet here in this dream Christ and Buddha are equal prophets."

While Millie continues to wrestle with her feelings of unworthiness, she is comforted by this mystical experience. She has worked hard to be grounded and is afraid that encountering the mystic in herself will upset what she has gained. She finally concludes, "If you follow the gifts of Christ, which are love and peace, and the example of Buddha teaching gentle discipline, then this leads to healing. If you follow these gifts, it still doesn't mean you won't be beaten up in the world, but there's a place to go to be healed."

Michael, a very creative, work-driven entrepreneur, had this vision quest dream while starting his new business. The dream had two scenes.

"In the first, *two middle-aged Indian men are on a spiritual quest. They carry nothing and travel fast through the wild, followed by a lion.*

They enter a tunnel to get away. One goes on, while the other stays behind, trying to maneuver an upholstered chair without cushions between him and the lion. It doesn't work. As the lion comes up to smell him, a bear ambles up and grabs the lion with his claws on either side of his hips. The Indian runs down the tunnel, silently thanking his totem for saving his life.

Michael describes the second scene,

"*Two medics are carrying the torn and bloody remains of an ostrich on a stretcher into an infirmary. The lion has killed the ostrich.*"

Awaking, Michael was determined to change the dream's conclusion. He wanted to see what would happen if he chose another way of acting. So, imagining himself as the Indian who had run away, he chose to stand and face the lion, who was being held by the bear. He heard the bear say, "The lion is not ready to be with you. Wait." The lion sniffed him as he stood still. He slowly scratched the lion's head. Immediately Michael understood that the Indian man had run down the tunnel because he misperceived the lion's intentions. The lion was merely curious, not menacing. Michael said, "I am enveloped in his power, the power of curiosity without a tinge of fear, the power that can cope with anything."

As Michael continued to work with the lion, he realized how alike he and the lion were. The lion raged and was furious with the ostrich. Michael is critical of ostrich-like people, who may appear stupid and incompetent. He also dislikes those who do not treat him well, or who do not see things as he does. He treats himself like an ostrich, too. "I goad myself to be what I am not, veering off into fear of the lion."

This dream led Michael to explore his personal power and to find a place for it to take root. He reentered the dream and found himself in a cave with the lion, stroking its head. The lion grabbed Michael's arm in his jaws and pulled him from the cave into the world. Michael walked beside him, a hand on his shoulder. With the lion beside him, he thought, "Nothing can harm me. I can deal with life from strength and consciousness. I can cease to be fear-driven. I can let pettiness fade."

The lion was truly Michael's deepest self, which does not fear humiliation and which speaks and acts without censorship. "Strength begets strength. Giving strength gives strength to life. The lion calls me to walk like it, deep in the earth, focused downward to my core and the strength that comes from it. The challenge is to stay connected to the lion. To find a practice to keep me in touch with it is like walking down into the ground. I separated too early from my mother and father, and scattered myself into the world. Now the task is to harvest these aspects and grow whole. The lion is the key. He guides me and models wholeness. Each discomfort is a path to finding and reclaiming another fragment of myself. When I hit a wall, inner or outer, the question is not how I can hold my place and be whole, but rather how I can use it to become more whole."

With these realizations, Michael knew he had begun to speak like the bear, whose wisdom balances the lion's unbridled action. "I need both wisdom and action, but I wasn't ready for both when I first had the dream."

As Michael moved toward this vision of wholeness, he heard his father's voice, speaking Yiddish. "Vu geunisht helpen." (A cry of despair, literally meaning "nothing will help you.") Michael knew this as the voice of hopelessness, where the ostrich hides its head in the ground and no vision is possible. Because one cannot see very far in fog, it is easy to succumb to the voice of despair and fear. Michael recognized this old response, so he chose to reenter the dream at this place.

"The lion blows the fog away and I see dark, blocky shapes on rolling hills. I approach one. Black marble slabs, freestanding with bases buried in the earth. Large slabs placed on top form the roof. Within I sense a coiled vibrant life. I begin to chisel an opening, following a spiral pattern outward from the center, slowly deepening the channel until I break through the slab, until I can meet and join with what is within."

This vision quest dream runs like a thread through Michael's inner life as he works with it in a variety of ways: going back into the dream and letting it unfold, meditating, journal writing, and sharing the ongoing dream with his therapist.

"I am becoming the lion in my business, grounded in action that has purpose and takes risks and that acts from a place that is true to myself. With the lion leading me, I am content to follow step-by-step. I can't see very far, but I trust where my wiser self leads. I'm just learning about the bear and where he fits into this picture. I don't have a sense yet, but I'm not rushing it. I feel a tremendous depth here that will keep coming as I follow it. There is still more to uncover. There's the tunnel, the chair, the Indians. Maybe I will work with them. Maybe I won't."

Seen from the outside, it is not always evident which dreams are full of spiritual power. These dreams must be experienced in order to know that you are in the presence of a greater power. Only you the dreamer know this. Frank, Millie and Michael all knew they had had powerful dreams, dreams that altered their lives. Often what has shifted takes time to be assimilated before the results are manifest. In my case the dream of awe which I dreamed in Languedoc, France was also a prescient dream, one which became manifest on the level of my physical and emotional reality seven years after I dreamed it.

Watch for these dreams. When you have one, nourish it: Carry it in your heart. Know that its vision will one day be manifest in your life.

Continuing the Journey

Is my soul asleep?
Have those beehives that labor
at night stopped? And the water
wheel of thought,
is it dry, the cups empty,
wheeling, carrying only shadows?

No, my soul is not asleep.
It is awake, wide awake.
It neither sleeps nor dreams, but watches,
its eyes wide open
far-off things, and listens
at the shores of the great silence.

—Antonio Machado
Translated by Robert Bly

Dreaming is one of those unexpected blessings of being alive. Each morning when we awaken we have the opportunity of remembering revelations of the night. No matter how many times we lay down to sleep, there is a boundary between waking and sleeping that we cross each time. We close our eyes. We rest our bodies. We drift into the place where dreams reside. Waking, we realize what a mystery sleep is. As we have surrendered to the Unknown, the Unknown has spoken to us in dreams come to light the way along our particular path.

It seems fitting that the final dream of this book be about dreams. As I came to the end of writing this book, I was thinking about liminal space, which comes from the Latin root word *limen*, literally the doorsill or threshold, and means the transitional stage of a process. What had first caught my eye was a footnote in *The Soul of Rumi* in which Coleman Barks says, "Rumi's poetry moves in a liminal space, an area between worlds." I wanted to know liminal space in a visceral way. I wanted to know if dreams also are of this space.

Then I dreamed of *a woman going on a journey. In preparation she enters her tower and takes the elevator up to the 10th floor. She decides to stop on the second floor to see the accounts department and get money for the journey, but a woman in the elevator starts telling her a joke, so she decides to ride to the top in order to hear the whole joke and then stop on the second floor on the way out of the tower.*

When she gets to the 10th floor, she runs a steamy bath and looks at pictures of her own private symbols, which move automatically as if they are on videotape. The steamy water and her private imagery evoke liminal space. Here the light is different, brassy; it has a surreal quality. Mixed with the steam, her images glare in that light. They seem to have no connection to one another except in evoking her internal space. They are a slowed-down dream.

Personally, this dream speaks to one of my struggles in life: creating a balance between *doing* and *being*. I am often overly conscientious about the pragmatic, "accounting" aspects of my life, and forget to dwell in the spacious place within. I can give precedence to tasks, taking life too seriously and forget to notice the humor of it. I can become too involved in the task at hand and forget to give myself solitude. The tower in this dream reminds me of the tower at Bollingen, which Carl Jung built for himself on the upper part of Lake Zurich in Switzerland. It was his place of solitude, his refuge. He wrote, "Solitude is a fount of healing, which makes my life worth living."

I felt that this dream was also given as guidance for those who will read this book. Receiving all that our dreams have to give depends upon our willingness to seclude ourselves. As a reminder of just how important this is, in a synchronistic moment during the editing of this chapter, I heard Ella Fitzgerald singing Duke Ellington's words: "Here in my seclusion . . . drifting, dreaming in an azure interlude."

Are we willing to seclude ourselves in order to explore the dream in the space between activities? The dream comes to us in the deep solitude of sleep, when the ego is silenced. But even in waking hours there is a need for quiet and spaciousness in order to open to the wisdom of the dream.

This dream was an answer to my desire to experience liminal space. There, I am no longer where I was before and have not yet arrived where I am going. I stand on the threshhold.

At the time of completing this book, I found myself on the threshold in several areas of my life. I was about to begin a new journey or phase. I had recently ended a long therapy, and was entering my sixties. I knew that the publication of this book would lead me further into the world in ways I could not predict. And I was looking for the right words with which to close all these ending chapters of my life and this book.

I have spoken to you about the path of awakening, enriched and guided by nightly dreams. I have offered you tools to gather and explore them. I still want to ask the question: what are these experiences in the night, the ones we call dreams?

In the words and sensorial experience of this dream, I know that our dreams are a language of their own with a surreal quality; we see them in a light both misty and brassy. Full of images that seem to have no connection to one another, they evoke our soul's world. To understand them and allow them to replenish us, we have to rise above our outer world concerns.

With dreams, we are face-to-face with liminal space, another way of describing Mystery, the place of possibility outside the usual boundaries of time and space. What the dream requires of us to make sense of it are emptiness and receptivity. We do not come to the dream to imprint upon it our ego's explanations or intentions. We come to receive our soul's awareness.

This dream had a second part, which evokes another question. *After being in the dream space of the 10th floor, I descend to the bottom floor where my baby is. One wall of this room with high ceilings can be opened sideways to reveal a snow capped mountain and alpine stream. The other people in the room start to close it, but I feel claustrophobic and say, "No, I need to see the vistas." They leave it open a couple of inches so I can breathe. Later I notice chill bumps on my friend's arm and realize how cold she is. By this time I feel settled, so we close the wall.*

How do we go back and forth between the dreamworld and the waking world? How can we integrate dream wisdom into daily life?

The journey of consciousness begins on the material level (getting money for the journey). Curiosity carries us to where our dreams can be seen for what they really are, as glimpses into our interior lives. This space is our own, but we cannot remain here indefinitely. There comes a time to rejoin the human community where we need to consider others and be willing to compromise. But even here we do not have to give up the vistas of our dreams. We may have to close the window at times, but when we feel claustrophobic, bound by the earth, all we have to do is open it again.

As you work with your dreams and devote yourself to awakening to all of yourself, you create a living relationship with your soul. The dream is the face of the Beloved. You will dream, remember, forget, return, struggle and embrace the Beloved. Such is the nature of relationship.

Our sleeping and our dreams will be with us until we take our last great sleep; they also prepare us for whatever comes after this life. They are our bread from heaven, our manna or sustenance. Each night when we enter into sleep, we descend into the unknown; as we do this, our dreams ascend to meet us. Then each morning when we awaken, we greet them and begin the process of understanding and living them.

This is a journey rich with healing opportunities. As we spiral inward in search of the true self, there is no one who knows us better, no one we can trust more than our soul. The Divine is unlimited. We are the limiters. At the same time we are amazing human beings. For a moment consider the complexity of the systems in our bodies, hidden from view, yet working in a sophisticated pattern of relationship. Consider our brains capable of endless learning and creativity. Consider our dreams; with the exception of the recurring dream, no two dreams are the same. Consider how sleep has been built into all creatures who live on the earth. Sleep enables us to rest and gives us the blessing of endlessly creative dreams. Jungian analyst and author Marion Woodman has said that every time we lie down to sleep, God prepares a magnificent feast of dreams for us. Each time we ignore our dreams, we pass up the feast. As long as we are alive, the promise of new dreams and unexplored inner and outer vistas is ours.

At the beginning of *Awakening the Dreamer* I set out to be your guide. Now that you have a map for the journey, my hope for you is that you feast on your dreams. Become a conscious dreamer: Take your dreams seriously, love their creativity, listen to the voice of your soul as it guides you, and strive to become your deepest self. Seek helpers to assist you in unraveling the meanings of your dreams. And as you develop your own gift of dreamwork, pass it on.

Acknowledgments

I am deeply grateful to all those who enrich and bless my life and who have supported the creation of this book. Without you my life and this book would not as rich.

Michael Bratnick, my beloved husband and fellow traveler. Marjorie Bair, my dear friend, who meticulously edited my manuscript, challenging me to be as precise as possible. Arlene Shulman, Carolyn Tilove, and Eileen Marder-Mirman, whose love and friendship have made all the difference in my life.

Kenneth Porter, who helped me trust my work and saw the power of my relationship with those who come to me for healing. Jason Shulman, my dear friend, who became my teacher. He saw what was possible and then showed me how to embody new dimensions of consciousness.

Liz Davidson and John Ballantyne, artists and engaging dreamers who invited me to give dream and imaginal workshops in their home in Canada. It was there that I dreamed of the Seven Sleepers and found the direction for this book. The conscious dreamers who willingly shared their intimate processes with me and thus with the readers. All my students and clients, who engage with me in discovering the wisdom of their dreams. Their trust, willingness and openness about revealing their deep selves have been a gift for me as well as for them.

Gayle Seminara-Mandel and Julie Fedeli, whose support for and input to this book were very valuable. Lynne McLewin who generously proofread the manuscript.

ACKNOWLEDGMENTS

Kim Sommer, Suzanne Harris, Judi Bachrach, Susan Harris, Judy Sirota-Rosenthal and Eve Marie Elkin-Schaffer, who at various junctures in the creation of this book gave me a loving and helpful boost.

Stephanie and Ann Julia, my daughters who follow adventurous paths and dream strong dreams. David Tilove, Jamie Mirman, Barry Guthertz, Mary Moross, and my fellow IKH colleagues, whom I know I can always call upon.

Scott Wilson and Nicole Maffei for giving this book the physical form to match its message.

My dream and creative/art teachers: Dr. Francis X. Clifton, Madame Colette Muscat (teacher of my dream teachers), Brenda Goldman, Joan Klutch, Aviva Gold, Marguerite Brennan, Judith Cornell and Deborah Koff-Chapin.

Two poets whose writings nourished me during the process of creating this book: William Stafford and Rumi. Though I was never privileged to meet William Stafford, his poetry and philosophy of writing and living are so accessible that I have seen and taken courage from his life. Through Coleman Barks' exquisite translations of Rumi, I have continually been brought into the presence of the greater dream.

Further Reading and Resources

DREAMS

Barasch, Marc Ian. *Healing Dreams*. New York: Riverhead Books, 2000.
Bosnak, Robert. *A Little Course in Dreams*. Boston: Shambhala, 1988.
_____. *Tracks in the Wilderness of Dreaming*. New York: Delta, 1996.
Bradshaw, John. "Integrating Your Disowned Parts," *Healing the Shame that Binds You*. Deerfield Beach, FL: Health Communications, Inc., 1988.
Epel, Naomi. *Writers Dreaming*. New York: Carol Southern Books, 1993.
Foreman, Ellen. *Awakening: A Dream Journal*. New York: Steward, Tabori & Chang, 1988.
Frankiel, Tamar and Judy Greenfield. *Entering the Temple of Dreams*. Woodstock, VT: Jewish Lights Publishing, 2000.
Garfield, Patricia. *Creative Dreaming*. New York: Ballantine Books, 1974.
Godwin, Malcolm. *The Lucid Dreamer*. New York: A Labyrinth Book, Simon and Schuster, 1994.
Guiley, Rosemary Ellen. *Dreamwork for the Soul*. New York: Berkeley Books, 1998.
Hagan, James. *Diamonds of the Night: The Search for Spirit in Your Dreams*. Berkeley, CA: PageMill Press, 1997.
Hoffman, Edward. "Six Keys of Kabbalistic Dreamwork," *Opening the Inner Gates*. Boston: Shambhala, 1995.
Jaffe, Aniela, ed. *C.G. Jung Word and Image*. Princeton, NJ: Princeton University Press, 1979.
Johnson, Robert A. *Inner Work*. San Francisco: Harper & Row, 1986.
Jung, C.G. *Memories, Dreams, Reflections*. New York: Vintage Books, 1965.
_____. "Concerning Rebirth," from *Encountering Jung on Death and Immortality*. Selected and Introduced by Jenny Yates. Princeton, NJ: Princeton University Press, 1999.
Lauck, Marcia S. and Deborah Koff-Chapin. *At the Pool of Wonder*. Santa Fe, NM: Bear & Company, 1989.
Mellick, Jill. *The Natural Artistry of Dreams*. Berkeley, CA: Conari Press, 1996.
_____. *The Art of Dreaming*. Berkeley, CA: Conari Press, 2001.
Moss, Robert. *Conscious Dreaming*. New York: Crown Trade Paperbacks, 1996.
_____. *Dreamgates*. New York: Three Rivers Press, 1998.
_____. *Dreaming True*. New York: Pocket Books, 2000.
Noble, Vicki. "The Dreamer and Her Path of Power," *Shakti Woman*. New York: HarperSanFrancisco, 1991.

Russack, Neil. *Animal Guides: In Life, Myth & Dreams*. Toronto: Inner City Books, 2002.
Sanford, John A. *Dreams and Healing*. Mahwah, NJ: Paulist Press, 1978.
———. *Dreams: God's Forgotten Language*. New York: HarperSanFrancisco, 1968, 1989.
Singer, June. *Boundaries of the Soul*. New York: Doubleday, rev. ed., 1994.
Van de Castle, Robert L. *Our Dreaming Mind*. New York: Ballantine Books, 1994.

THE CREATIVE LIFE

Allen, Pat B. *Art is a Way of Knowing*. Boston: Shambhala, 1995.
Arguelles, Jose and Miriam. *Mandala*. Boston: Shambhala, 1985.
Bennett, Hal Zina. *Write from the Heart*. Mill Valley, CA: Nataraj Publishing, 1995.
Bolen, Jean Shinoda. *Crossing to Avalon*. New York, HarperCollins, 1994.
Cassou, Michele and Stewart Cubley. *Life, Paint and Passion*. New York: Jeremy P. Tarcher/Putnam, 1995.
Colegrave, Sukie. *By Way of Pain: A Passage into Self*. Rochester, NY: Park Street Press, 1988.
Cornell, Judith. *Mandala: Luminous Symbols for Healing*. Wheaton, IL: Quest Books, 1994.
Diaz, Adriana. *Freeing the Creative Spirit*. New York: HarperSanFrancisco, 1992.
Fincher, Susanne F. *Creating Mandalas*. Boston: Shambhala, 1991.
Fox, John. *Finding What You Didn't Lose*. New York: G. P. Putnam's Sons, 1995.
Ganim, Barbara and Susan Fox. *Visual Journaling*. Wheaton, IL: Quest Books, 1999.
Gold, Aviva. *Painting from the Source*. New York: Harper Collins, 1998.
Hinchman, Hannah. *A Life in Hand: Creating the Illuminated Journal*. Salt Lake City, UT: Peregrine Smith Books, 1991.
Kent, Corita & Jan Steward. *Learning by Heart*. New York: Bantam Books, 1992.
Koff-Chapin, Deborah. *Drawing Out Your Soul: The Touch Drawing Handbook*. Langley, WA: Center for Touch Drawing. 1999.
Lamott, Anne. *Bird by Bird*. New York: Anchor Books, Doubleday, 1994.
Malchiodi, Cathy A. *The Soul's Palette: Drawing on Art's Transformative Powers for Health and Well-Being*. Boston: Shambhala, 2002.
Metzger, Deena. *Writing for Your Life*. New York: HarperSanFrancisco, 1992.
Richards, M.C. *Centering*. Hanover, NH: Wesleyan University Press, 1989.
Rilke, Rainer Maria. *Letters to a Young Poet*. Translated by Stephen Mitchell. New York: Vintage Books, 1984.

FURTHER READING AND RESOURCES

SYMBOLS

Cooper, J.C. *An Illustrated Encyclopaedia of Traditional Symbols*. London: Thames and Hudson, 1978.
Fontana, David. *The Secret Language of Symbols*. San Francisco: Chronicle Books, 1993.
Matthews, Boris, trans. *The Herder Symbol Dictionary*. Wilmette, IL: Chiron Publications, 1986.

POETRY

Berry, Wendell. *Collected Poems*. New York: North Point Press, Farrar, Straus and Giroux, 1985.
Bly, Robert. *The Soul is Here for Its Own Joy: Sacred Poems from Many Cultures*. Hopewell, NJ: The Ecco Press, 1995.
Collins. Billy. *Picnic, Lightning*. Pittsburgh, PA: University of Pittsburgh Press, 1998.
Holabird, Jean. *Out of the Ruins—A New York Record*. Coste Madera, CA: Gingko Press, 2002.
Kabir. *The Kabir Book*, versions by Robert Bly. Boston: The Seventies Press, 1977.
Kenyon, Jane. *The Boat of Quiet Hours*. Saint Paul, MN: Graywolf Press, 1986.
Lalla. *Naked Song*. Translated by Coleman Barks. Atlanta, GA: Maypop Books, 1992.
Lee, Li-Young. *Book of My Nights*. Rochester, NY: BOA Editions Ltd., 2001.
Machado, Antonio. *Times Alone: Selected Poems of Antonio Machado*, translated by Robert Bly. Middletown, CT: Wesleyan University Press, 1983.
Neruda, Pablo. *The Sea and the Bells*. Translated by William O'Daly. Port Townsend, WA: Copper Canyon Press, 1988.
———. *The Book of Questions*. Translated by William O'Daly. Port Townsend, WA: Copper Canyon Press, 1991.
Oliver, Mary. *New And Selected Poems*. Boston, MA: Beacon Press, 1992.
Richards, M.C. *Imagine Inventing Yellow*. Barrytown, NY: Station Hill, 1991.
Rilke, Rainer Maria. *The Selected Poetry of Rainer Maria Rilke*. Edited and translated by Stephen Mitchell. New York: Vintage Books, 1989.
Rilke, Rainer Maria. *Book of Hours*. Translated by Anita Barrows and Joanna Macy. New York: Riverhead Books, 1996.
Rumi. *The Essential Rumi*. Translated by Coleman Barks. New York: HarperSanFrancisco, 1995.
———. *The Soul of Rumi*. New York: HarperSanFrancisco, 2001.
Stafford, William. *An Oregon Message*. New York: HarperCollins Publishers, 1987.
———. *Even in Quiet Places*. Lewiston, ID: Confluence Press, 1996.
———. *My Name is William Tell*. Lewiston, ID: Confluence Press, 1992.
———. *Passwords*. New York: HarperCollins Publishers, 1991.

FURTHER READING AND RESOURCES

_____. *The Way It Is*. St. Paul, MN: Graywolf Press, 1998.
Whyte, David. *Fire in the Earth*. Langley, WA: Many Rivers Press, 1992.
_____. *The House of Belonging*. Langley, WA: Many Rivers Press, 1997.
_____. *Where Many Rivers Meet*. Langley, WA: Many Rivers Press, 1993.

ADDITIONAL READINGS

Bryant, Dorothy. *The Kin of Ata Are Waiting for You*. New York: Random House; Berkeley, CA : Moon Books, 1971.

Estes, Clarissa Pinkola. *Women Who Run with the Wolves*. New York, NY: Ballantine Books, 1992.

James, Van. *Spirit and Art*. Great Barrington, MA: Anthroposophic Press, 2001.

Johnson, Robert A. *Balancing Heaven and Earth: A Memoir*. New York: HarperSanFrancisco, 1998.

Klinkenborg, Verlyn, "Awakening to Sleep," *The New York Times Magazine*, January 5, 1997.

Luke, Helen M. *Such Stuff as Dreams Are Made On*. New York: Parabola Books, 2000.

Perera, Sylvia Brinton. *Descent to the Goddess*. Toronto, Canada: Inner City Books, 1981.

Pierrakos, Eva. "The Evolutionary Process," and "Three Aspects that Prevent Loving," The Pathwork Foundation.

RESOURCES

A Society of Souls® (a school for Integrated Kabbalistic Healing®); IM™ (Impersonal Movement, a body-centered practice); and The Work of Return™, (a self-healing practice). Call (973) 538-7689 or website: www.kabbalah.org

Association for the Study of Dreams, (annual conference, workshops, and newsletter) P.O. Box 1600, Vienna, Va. 22183; website: *www.ASDreams.org*

Center for Intentional Living (psycho-spiritual experiential learning community in Salem, NY). Website: www.intentionalliving.com

Deborah Koff-Chapin's Center for Touch Drawing. Call 800-989-6334 or website: www.touchdrawing.com

Interweave (a Learning Center in Summit, NJ, for Wellness, Spirituality & the Common Good). Website: www.interweave.org

The Pathwork (a spiritual path of transformation). Website: www.pathwork.org

Index

1. CREATIVE EXERCISES

Active Imagination	113
Becoming the Symbol	119
Collage	134
Tissue paper	135
Collection of dreams	177
Dramatization with a Group	210
Dream Painting	122
Epitaph of a Dream Character	143
Free Association	112
Free Writing	138
If It Were My Dream	207
Mandala	127, 130
Inspiraling	131
Autobiographical	133
Meditation	145
Mixed Media	136
Movement	146
Poetry	140
Sculpture	136
Story from a Collection of Dreams	178
Touch Drawing	180
Wheel of Association	202

INDEX

2. EXERCISES FOR WORKING WITH DREAMS

Completing a Dream	80
Conscious Intention	48
Creating a Collection of Dreams	175
Creating a Dream Community	197
Creating a Ritual Practice	93
Enhancing Dream Recall	79
Finding Your Dream Rhythm	64
Incubation	159
In-Depth Exploration of a Dream	71
Each character and object an aspect of dreamer	72
Keeping a daily review	73
Learning the Art of Listening	199
Listening to the dream's questions	71
Trusting your feelings and intuition	75
Initial Exploration of a Dream.	69
Keeping a Journal	67
Making a Conscious Intention	47
Working with Resistance	
Despair	98
Distrusting inactivity.	162
Doubt	97
Dream fragments	77
Exposing your intimate self to others.	194
Fighting the unknown	163
Flood of dreams	81
Forgotten dreams	79
Forgetting a dream practice	96
Handling personality conflicts in a dream group	195
Incomplete dreams	80
"I'm not an artist or writer"	108
Judgments	96
"My dreams are too ugly and painful"	109
Necessary resistance	110
Resistance to dreamwork	50
Resistance to intention	53
Resistance to Working with the Collection	182

3. IMAGINAL JOURNEYS AND MEDITATIONS

Active Imagination	113
Connecting with Your Soul's Desire	231
Dream Community	233
Finding an Intention	49
Incubating a Dream	230
Inductions to Imaginal Journeys	224, 225
Meditating on a Dream	145
Slumbering Seeds	232
The Seven Sleepers	12, 227

The author wishes to thank the following for permission to reprint portions of the works indicated:

"Sleeping Toward Heaven" and "Querencia" copyright © 1987 William Stafford from *Oregon Message* (Harper and Row). "The Dream of Now" copyright © 1991 from *Passwords* (HarperCollins). Reprinted by permission of The Estate of William Stafford.

Excerpts from *Times Alone: Selected Poems of Antonio Machado*, translated by Robert Bly, Wesleyan University Press, Middletown, CT, 1983, copyright © 1983 Robert Bly. Reprinted with his permission.

From *Inner Work* by Robert A. Johnson, copyright © 1986 by Robert A. Johnson. Reprinted with permission of HarperCollins Publishers Inc.

Excerpt from *Naked Song* by Lalla, translated by Coleman Barks, Maypop Books, copyright © 1992 Coleman Barks. Reprinted with his permission.

"In Impossible Darkness" by Kim Rosen. Reprinted with her permission.

Excerpts from "The Dream That Must Be Interpreted," *The Essential Rumi* (copyright © 2001 Coleman Barks) and "Blade," *The Soul of Rumi* (copyright © 1995 Coleman Barks), both translated by Coleman Barks. Reprinted with his permission.

"At Lascaux" is reprinted with the permission of Confluence Press from *My Name is William Tell*, copyright © 1992 by William Stafford.

Excerpt from *The Book of Qualities* by J. Ruth Gendler, copyright © 1984 Janet Ruth Gendler. Reprinted with permission of HarperCollins Publishers Inc.

Excerpts from Eva Pierrakos used by permission of The Pathwork® Foundation, 13013 Collingwood Terrace, Silver Spring, MD 20904-1414.

Excerpt from "Perhaps While Dreaming," by Antonio Machado from an unpublished translation by David Whyte. Used by permission of David Whyte.

Exerpt from "Faith" in *Where Many Rivers Meet* by David Whyte, copyright © 1990 by David Whyte. Used by permission of the author and Many Rivers Press.

"The Seeds" from *Collected Poems* by Wendell Berry, copyright © 1985 by Wendell Berry. Reprinted by permission of North Point Press, a division of Farrar, Straus and Giroux, LLC.

"Where is the Child I Was?" from Pablo Neruda's *The Book of Questions*, copyright © 1991 by William O'Daly, tr., reprinted by permission of Copper Canyon Press.

ABOUT THE AUTHOR

Raechel Bratnick is a dream guide, psychotherapist and healer. An adept in the language of dreams in the tradition of the biblical Joseph, she leads workshops, courses and dream communities using her unique approach to exploring and communicating with dreams in their own language.

She has trained in a number of psychological and spiritual modalities, which include the groundbreaking waking dream therapy of Madame Colette Muscat; the Center for Intentional Living's synthesis of depth and transpersonal psychologies; the Pathwork; and Integrated Kabbalistic Healing® (IKH), developed by the modern Kabbalist Jason Shulman; she also studied Jungian dreamwork. Her work in a variety of creative forms—painting, pottery, mandala, poetry, touch drawing and sandplay—inform her personal and professional explorations. As a healer of body, mind and spirit, she now joins her calling with dreams and the creative arts to her understanding of the depth psychologies and the IKH diagnostic process.

Raechel was raised in Moscow, Idaho, where she received her B.A. and M.A. from the University of Idaho. Prior to training as a psychotherapist in the 70s, she taught college English; then as a Vice President in a major communications agency in New York City, she directed public relations campaigns for publishers and the medical community. She has also written children's stories and plays.

She has a private practice working with teenagers, adults and couples in Basking Ridge, and teaches at Interweave in Summit, both in New Jersey. She and her husband of 25 years, Michael, are the parents of Ann Julia and Stephanie Bratnick.

She welcomes communication from readers through the website www.awakeningthedreamer.com.

BVG